Good Sense

Baron D'Holbach

Contents

GOOD SENSE

BY

Baron D'Holbach

GOOD SENSE WITHOUT GOD:
OR
FREETHOUGHTS OPPOSED TO SUPERNATURAL IDEAS
A TRANSLATION OF BARON D'HOLBACH'S "LE BON SENS"

> "*Atheism* leaves men to Sense, to Philosophy, to Laws, to Reputation, all which may be guides to moral Virtue, tho' Religion were not: but Superstition dismounts all these, and erects an absolute Monarchy in the Minds of Men. Therefore, Atheism did never perturb States; but Superstition hath been the confusion of many. The causes of Superstition are pleasing and sensual rights, and Ceremonies; Excess of Pharisaical and outside holiness, Reverence to Traditions and the stratagems of Prelates for their own Ambition and Lucre."

-- Lord Bacon.

PUBLISHER'S NOTE

THE chief design in reprinting this translation, is to preserve "*the strongest atheistical work*" for present and future generations of English Freethinkers. The real author was, unquestionably, Paul Thyry; Baron D'Holbach, and not John Meslier, to whom this work has been wrongly attributed, under the title of "Le Bon Sens" (Common Sense).

In 1770, Baron D'Holbach published his masterpiece, "Systeme de la Nature," which for a long time passed as the posthumous work of M. de Mirabaud. That text-book of "Atheistical Philosophy" caused a great sensation, and two years later, 1772, the Baron published this excellent abridgment of it, freed from arbitrary ideas; and by its clearness of expression, facility, and precision of style, rendered it most suitable for the average student.

"Le Bon Sens" was privately printed in Amsterdam, and the author's name was kept a profound secret; hence, Baron D'Holbach escaped persecution.

THE AUTHOR'S PREFACE

When we examine the opinions of men, we find that nothing is more uncommon, than common sense; or, in other words, they lack judgment to discover plain truths, or to reject absurdities, and palpable contradictions. We have an example of this in Theology, a system revered in all countries by a great number of men; an object regarded by them as most important, and indispensable to happiness. An examination of the principles upon which this pretended system is founded, forces us to acknowledge, that these principles are only suppositions, imagined by ignorance, propagated by enthusiasm or knavery, adopted by timid credulity, preserved by custom which never reasons, and revered solely because not understood.

In a word, whoever uses common sense upon religious opinions, and will bestow on this inquiry the attention that is commonly given to most subjects, will easily perceive that Religion is a mere castle in the air. Theology is ignorance of natural causes; a tissue of fallacies and contradictions. In every country, it presents romances void of probability, the hero of which is composed of impossible qualities. His name, exciting fear in all minds, is only a vague word, to which, men affix ideas or qualities, which are either contradicted by facts, or inconsistent.

Notions of this being, or rather, *the word* by which he is designated, would be a matter of indifference, if it did not cause innumerable ravages in the world. But men, prepossessed with the opinion that this phantom is a reality of the greatest interest, instead of concluding wisely from its incomprehensibility, that they are not bound to regard it, infer on the contrary, that they must contemplate it, without ceasing, and never lose sight of it. Their invincible ignorance, upon this subject, irritates their curiosity; instead of putting them upon guard against their imagination, this ignorance renders them decisive, dogmatic, imperious, and even exasperates them against all, who oppose doubts to the reveries which they have begotten.

What perplexity arises, when it is required to solve an insolvable problem; unceasing meditation upon an object, impossible to understand, but in which however he thinks himself much concerned, cannot but excite man, and produce a fever in his brain. Let interest, vanity, and ambition, co-operate ever so little with this unfortunate turn of mind, and society must necessarily be disturbed. This is the reason that so many nations have often been the scene of extravagances of senseless visionaries, who, believing their empty speculations to be eternal truths, and publishing them as such, have kindled the zeal of princes and their subjects, and made them take up arms for opinions, represented to them as essential to the glory of the Deity. In all parts of our globe, fanatics have cut each other's throats, publicly burnt each other, committed without a scruple and even as a duty, the greatest crimes, and shed torrents of blood. For what? To strengthen, support, or propagate the impertinent conjectures of some enthusiasts, or to give validity to the cheats of impostors, in the name of a being, who exists only in their imagination, and who has made himself known only by the ravages, disputes, and follies, he has caused.

Savage and furious nations, perpetually at war, adore, under divers names, some God, conformable to their ideas, that is to say, cruel, carnivorous, selfish, blood-thirsty. We find, in all the religions, "a God of armies," a "jealous God," an "avenging God," a "destroying God," a "God," who is pleased with carnage, and whom his worshippers consider it a duty to serve. Lambs, bulls, children, men, and women, are sacrificed to him. Zealous servants of this barbarous God think themselves obliged even to offer up themselves as a sacrifice to him. Madmen may everywhere be seen, who, after meditating upon their terrible God, imagine that to please him they must inflict on themselves, the most exquisite torments. The gloomy ideas formed of the deity, far from consoling them, have every where disquieted their minds, and prejudiced follies destructive to happiness.

How could the human mind progress, while tormented with frightful phantoms, and guided by men, interested in perpetuating its ignorance and fears? Man has been forced to vegetate in his primitive stupidity: he has been taught stories about invisible powers upon whom his happiness was supposed to depend. Occupied solely by his fears, and by unintelligible reveries, he has always been at the mercy of priests, who have reserved to themselves the right of thinking for him, and of directing his actions.

Thus, man has remained a slave without courage, fearing to reason, and unable to extricate himself from the labyrinth, in which he has been wandering. He believes himself forced under the yoke of his gods, known to him only by the fabulous accounts given by his ministers, who, after binding each unhappy mortal in the chains of prejudice, remain his masters, or else abandon him defenceless to the absolute power of tyrants, no less terrible than the gods, of whom they are the representatives.

Oppressed by the double yoke of spiritual and temporal power, it has been impossible for the people to be happy. Religion became sacred, and men have had no other Morality, than what their legislators and priests brought from the unknown regions of heaven. The human mind, confused by theological opinions, ceased to know its own powers, mistrusted experience, feared truth and disdained reason, in order to follow authority. Man has been a mere machine in the hands of tyrants and priests. Always treated as a slave, man has contracted the vices of slavery.

Such are the true causes of the corruption of morals. Ignorance and servitude are calculated to make men wicked and unhappy. Knowledge, Reason, and Liberty, can alone reform and make men happier. But every thing conspires to blind them, and to confirm their errors. Priests cheat them, tyrants corrupt and enslave them. Tyranny ever was, and ever will be, the true cause of man's depravity, and also of his calamities. Almost always fascinated by religious fiction, poor mortals turn not their eyes to the natural and obvious causes of their misery; but attribute their vices to the imperfection of their natures, and their unhappiness to the anger of the gods. They offer to heaven vows, sacrifices, and presents, to obtain the end of sufferings, which in reality, are attributable only to the negligence, ignorance, and perversity of their guides, to the folly of their customs, and above all, to the general want of knowledge. Let men's minds be filled with true ideas; let their reason be cultivated; and there will be no need of opposing to the passions, such a feeble barrier, as the fear of gods. Men will be good, when they are well instructed; and when they are despised for evil, or justly rewarded for good, which they do to their fellow citizens.

In vain should we attempt to cure men of their vices, unless we begin by curing them of their prejudices. It is only by showing them the truth, that they will perceive their true interests, and the real motives that ought to incline them to do good. Instructors have long enough fixed men's eyes upon heaven; let them now turn them upon earth. An incomprehensible theology, ridiculous fables, impenetrable mysteries, puerile ceremonies, are to be no longer endured. Let the human mind apply itself to what is natural, to intelligible objects, truth, and useful knowledge.

Does it not suffice to annihilate religious prejudice, to shew, that what is inconceivable to man, cannot be good for him? Does it require any thing, but plain common sense, to perceive, that a being, incompatible with the most evident notions--that a cause continually opposed to the effects which we attribute to it--that a being, of whom we can say nothing, without falling into contradiction--that a being, who, far from explaining the enigmas of the universe, only makes them more inexplicable--that a being, whom for so many ages men have vainly addressed to obtain their happiness, and the end of sufferings--does it require, I say, any thing but plain, common sense, to perceive--that the idea of such a being is an idea without model, and that he himself is merely a phantom of the imagination? Is any thing necessary but common sense to perceive, at least, that it is folly and madness for men to hate and damn one another about unintelligible opinions concerning a being of this kind? In short, does not every thing prove, that Morality and Virtue are totally incompatible with the notions of a God, whom his ministers and interpreters have described, in every country, as the most capricious, unjust, and cruel of tyrants, whose pretended will, however, must serve as law and rule the inhabitants of the earth?

To discover the true principles of Morality, men have no need of theology, of revelation, or of gods: They have need only of common sense. They have only to commune with themselves, to reflect upon their own nature, to consider the objects of society, and of the individuals, who compose it; and they will easily perceive, that virtue is advantageous, and vice disadvantageous to themselves. Let us persuade men to be just, beneficent, moderate, sociable; not because such conduct is demanded by the gods, but, because it is pleasant to men. Let us advise them to abstain from vice and crime; not because they will be punished in another world, but because they will suffer for it in this.-- *These are*, says Montesquieu, *means to prevent crimes--these are punishments; these reform manners-- these are good examples.*

The way of truth is straight; that of imposture is crooked and dark. Truth, ever necessary to man, must necessarily be felt by all upright minds; the lessons of reason are to be followed by all honest men. Men are unhappy, only because they are ignorant; they are ignorant, only because every thing conspires to prevent their being enlightened; they are wicked only because their reason is not sufficiently developed.

By what fatality then, have the first founders of all sects given to their gods ferocious characters, at which nature revolts? Can we imagine a conduct more abominable, than that which Moses tells us his God showed towards the Egyptians, where that assassin proceeds boldly to declare, in the name and by the order of *his God*, that Egypt shall be afflicted with the greatest calamities, that can happen to man? Of all the different ideas, which they give us of a supreme being, of a God, creator and preserver of mankind, there are none more horrible, than those of the impostors, who represented themselves as inspired by a divine spirit, and "Thus saith the Lord."

Why, O theologians! do you presume to inquire into the impenetrable mysteries of a being, whom you consider inconceivable to the human mind? You are the blasphemers, when you imagine that a being, perfect according to you, could be guilty of such cruelty towards creatures whom he has made out of nothing. Confess, your ignorance of a creating God; and cease meddling with mysteries, which are repugnant to *Common Sense*.

GOOD SENSE WITHOUT GOD

APOLOGUE

1. There is a vast empire, governed by a monarch, whose strange conduct is to confound the minds of his subjects. He wishes to be known, loved, respected, obeyed; but never shows himself to his subjects, and everything conspires to render uncertain the ideas formed of his character.

The people, subjected to his power, have, of the character and laws of their invisible sovereign, such ideas only, as his ministers give them. They, however, confess, that they have no idea of their master; that his ways are impenetrable; his views and nature totally incomprehensible. These ministers, likewise, disagree upon the commands which they pretend have been issued by the sovereign, whose servants they call themselves. They defame one another, and mutually treat each other as impostors and false teachers. The decrees and ordinances, they take upon themselves to promulgate, are obscure; they are enigmas, little calculated to be understood, or even divined, by the subjects, for whose instruction they were intended. The laws of the concealed monarch require interpreters; but the interpreters are always disputing upon the true manner of understanding them. Besides, they are not consistent with themselves; all they relate of their concealed prince is only a string of contradictions. They utter concerning him not a single word that does not immediately confute itself. They call him supremely good; yet many complain of his decrees. They suppose him infinitely wise; and under his administration everything appears to contradict reason. They extol his justice; and the best of his subjects are generally the least favoured. They assert, he sees everything; yet his presence avails nothing. He is, say they, the friend of order; yet throughout his dominions, all is in confusion and disorder. He makes all for himself; and the events seldom answer his designs. He foresees everything; but cannot prevent anything.

He impatiently suffers offence, yet gives everyone the power of offending him. Men admire the wisdom and perfection of his works; yet his works, full of imperfection, are of short duration. He is continually doing and undoing; repairing what he has made; but is never pleased with his work. In all his undertakings, he proposes only his own glory; yet is never glorified. His only end is the happiness of his subjects; and his subjects, for the most part want necessaries. Those, whom he seems to favour are generally least satisfied with their fate; almost all appear in perpetual revolt against a master, whose greatness they never cease to admire, whose wisdom to extol, whose goodness to adore, whose justice to fear, and whose laws to reverence, though never obeyed!

This EMPIRE is the WORLD; this MONARCH GOD; his MINISTERS are the PRIESTS; his SUBJECTS MANKIND.

2. There is a science that has for its object only things incomprehensible. Contrary to all other sciences, it treats only of what cannot fall under our senses. Hobbes calls it the *kingdom of darkness*. It is a country, where every thing is governed by laws, contrary to those which mankind are permitted to know in the world they inhabit. In this marvellous region, light is only darkness; evidence is doubtful or false; impossibilities are credible: reason is a deceitful guide; and good sense becomes madness. This *science* is called *theology*, and this theology is a continual insult to the reason of man.

3. By the magical power of "ifs," "buts," "perhaps's," "what do we know," etc., heaped together, a shapeless and unconnected system is formed, perplexing mankind, by obliterating from their minds, the most clear ideas and rendering uncertain truths most evident. By reason of this systematic confusion, nature is an enigma; the visible world has disappeared, to give place to regions invisible; reason is compelled to yield to imagination, who leads to the country of her self-invented chimeras.

4. The principles of every religion are founded upon the idea of a GOD. Now, it is impossible to have true ideas of a being, who acts upon none of our senses. All our ideas are representations of sensible objects. What then can represent to us the idea of God, which is evidently an idea without an object? Is not such an idea as impossible, as an effect without a cause? Can an idea without an archetype be anything, but a chimera? There are, however, divines, who assure us that the idea of God is innate; or that we have this idea in our mother's womb. Every principle

is the result of reason; all reason is the effect of experience; experience is acquired only by the exercise of our senses: therefore, religious principles are not founded upon reason, and are not innate.

5. Every system of religion can be founded only upon the nature of God and man; and upon the relations, which subsist between them. But to judge of the reality of those relations, we must have some idea of the divine nature. Now, the world exclaims, the divine nature is incomprehensible to man; yet ceases not to assign attributes to this incomprehensible God, and to assure us, that it is our indispensable duty to find out that God, whom it is impossible to comprehend.

The most important concern of man is what he can least comprehend. If God is incomprehensible to man, it would seem reasonable never to think of him; but religion maintains, man cannot with impunity cease a moment to think (or rather dream) of his God.

6. We are told, that divine qualities are not of a nature to be comprehended by finite minds. The natural consequence must be, that divine qualities are not made to occupy finite minds. But religion tells us, that the poor finite mind of man ought never to lose sight of an inconceivable being, whose qualities he can never comprehend. Thus, we see, religion is the art of turning the attention of mankind upon subjects they can never comprehend.

7. Religion unites man with God, or forms a communication between them; yet do they not say, God is infinite? If God be infinite, no finite being can have communication or relation with him. Where there is no relation, there can be no union, communication, or duties. If there be no duties between man and his God, there is no religion for man. Thus, in saying God is infinite, you annihilate religion for man, who is a finite being. The idea of infinity is to us an idea without model, without archetype, without object.

8. If God be an infinite being, there cannot be, either in the present or future world, any relative proportion between man and his God. Thus, the idea of God can never enter the human mind. In supposition of a life, in which man would be much more enlightened, than in this, the idea of the infinity of God would ever remain the same distance from his finite mind. Thus the idea of God will be no more clear in the future, than in the present life. Thus, intelligences, superior to man, can have no more complete ideas of God, than man, who has not the least conception of him

in his present life.

9. How has it been possible to persuade reasonable beings, that the thing, most impossible to comprehend, was most essential to them? It is because they have been greatly terrified; because, when they fear, they cease to reason; because, they have been taught to mistrust their own understanding; because, when the brain is troubled, they believe every thing, and examine nothing.

10. Ignorance and fear are the two hinges of all religion. The uncertainty in which man finds himself in relation to his God, is precisely the motive that attaches him to his religion. Man is fearful in the dark--in moral, as well as physical darkness. His fear becomes habitual, and habit makes it natural; he would think that he wanted something, if he had nothing to fear.

11. He, who from infancy has habituated himself to tremble when he hears pronounced certain words, requires those words and needs to tremble. He is therefore more disposed to listen to one, who entertains him in his fears, than to one, who dissuades him from them. The superstitious man wishes to fear; his imagination demands it; one might say, that he fears nothing so much, as to have nothing to fear.

Men are imaginary invalids, whose weakness empirics are interested to encourage, in order to have sale for their drugs. They listen rather to the physician, who prescribes a variety of remedies, than to him, who recommends good regimen, and leaves nature to herself.

12. If religion were more clear, it would have less charms for the ignorant, who are pleased only with obscurity, terrors, fables, prodigies, and things incredible. Romances, silly stories, and the tales of ghosts and wizards, are more pleasing to vulgar minds than true histories.

13. In point of religion, men are only great children. The more a religion is absurd and filled with wonders, the greater ascendancy it acquires over them. The devout man thinks himself obliged to place no bounds to his credulity; the more things are inconceivable, they appear to him divine; the more they are incredible, the greater merit, he imagines, there is in believing them.

14. The origin of religious opinions is generally dated from the time, when savage nations were yet in infancy. It was to gross, ignorant, and stupid people, that the founders of religion have in all ages addressed themselves, when they wished

to give them their Gods, their mode of worship, their mythology, their marvellous and frightful fables. These chimeras, adopted without examination by parents, are transmitted, with more or less alteration, to their children, who seldom reason any more than their parents.

15. The object of the first legislators was to govern the people; and the easiest method to effect it was to terrify their minds, and to prevent the exercise of reason. They led them through winding bye-paths, lest they might perceive the designs of their guides; they forced them to fix their eyes in the air, for fear they should look at their feet; they amused them on the way with idle stories; in a word, they treated them as nurses do children, who sing lullabies, to put them to sleep, and scold, to make them quiet.

16. The existence of a God is the basis of all religion. Few appear to doubt his existence; yet this fundamental article utterly embarrasses every mind that reasons. The first question of every catechism has been, and ever will be, the most difficult to resolve. (In the year 1701, the holy fathers of the oratory of Vendome maintained in a thesis, this proposition--that, according to St. Thomas, the existence of God is not, and cannot be, a subject of faith.)

17. Can we imagine ourselves sincerely convinced of the existence of a being, whose nature we know not; who is inaccessible to all our senses; whose attributes, we are assured, are incomprehensible to us? To persuade me that a being exists or can exist, I must be first told what that being is. To induce me to believe the existence or the possibility of such a being, it is necessary to tell me things concerning him that are not contradictory, and do not destroy one another. In short, to fully convince me of the existence of that being, it is necessary to tell me things that I can understand.

18. A thing is impossible, when it includes two ideas that mutually destroy one another, and which can neither be conceived nor united in thought. Conviction can be founded only upon the constant testimony of our senses, which alone give birth to our ideas, and enable us to judge of their agreement or disagreement. That, which exists necessarily, is that, whose non-existence implies a contradiction. These principles, universally acknowledged, become erroneous, when applied to the existence of a God. Whatever has been hitherto said upon the subject, is either unintelligible, or perfect contradiction, and must therefore appear absurd to every

rational man.

19. All human knowledge is more or less clear. By what strange fatality have we never been able to elucidate the science of God? The most civilized nations, and among them the most profound thinkers, are in this respect no more enlightened than the most savage tribes and ignorant peasants; and, examining the subject closely, we shall find, that, by the speculations and subtle refinements of men, the divine science has been only more and more obscured. Every religion has hitherto been founded only upon what is called, in logic, *begging the question*; it takes things for granted, and then proves, by suppositions, instead of principles.

20. Metaphysics teach us, that God is a *pure spirit*. But, is modern theology superior to that of the savages? The savages acknowledge a *great spirit*, for the master of the world. The savages, like all ignorant people, attribute to *spirits* all the effects, of which their experience cannot discover the true causes. Ask a savage, what works your watch? He will answer, *it is a spirit*. Ask the divines, what moves the universe? They answer, *it is a spirit*.

21. The savage, when he speaks of a spirit, affixes, at least, some idea to the word; he means thereby an agent, like the air, the breeze, the breath, that invisibly produces discernible effects. By subtilizing every thing, the modern theologian becomes as unintelligible to himself as to others. Ask him, what he understands by a spirit? He will answer you, that it is an unknown substance, perfectly simple, that has no extension, that has nothing common with matter. Indeed, is there any one, who can form the least idea of such a substance? What then is a spirit, to speak in the language of modern theology, but the absence of an idea? The idea of *spirituality* is an idea without model.

22. Is it not more natural and intelligible to draw universal existence from the matter, whose existence is demonstrated by all the senses, and whose effects we experience, which we see act, move, communicate motion, and incessantly generate, than to attribute the formation of things to an unknown power, to a spiritual being, who cannot derive from his nature what he has not himself, and who, by his spiritual essence, can create neither matter nor motion? Nothing is more evident, than that the idea they endeavour to give us, of the action of mind upon matter, represents no object. It is an idea without model.

23. The material *Jupiter* of the ancients could move, compose, destroy, and

create beings, similar to himself; but the God of modern theology is sterile. He can neither occupy any place in space, nor move matter, nor form a visible world, nor create men or gods. The metaphysical God is fit only to produce confusion, reveries, follies, and disputes.

24. Since a God was indispensably requisite to men, why did they not worship the Sun, that visible God, adored by so many nations? What being had greater claim to the homage of men, than the day-star, who enlightens, warms, and vivifies all beings; whose presence enlivens and regenerates nature, whose absence seems to cast her into gloom and languor? If any being announced to mankind, power, activity, beneficence, and duration, it was certainly the Sun, whom they ought to have regarded as the parent of nature, as the divinity. At least, they could not, without folly, dispute his existence, or refuse to acknowledge his influence.

25. The theologian exclaims to us, that God wants neither hands nor arms to act; that *he acts by his will*. But pray, who or what is that God, who has a will, and what can be the subject of his divine will?

Are the stories of witches, ghosts, wizards, hobgoblins, etc., more absurd and difficult to believe than the magical or impossible action of mind upon matter? When we admit such a God, fables and reveries may claim belief. Theologians treat men as children, whose simplicity makes them believe all the stories they hear.

26. To shake the existence of God, we need only to ask a theologian to speak of him. As soon as he has said a word upon the subject, the least reflection will convince us, that his observations are totally incompatible with the essence he ascribes to his God. What then is God? It is an abstract word, denoting the hidden power of nature; or it is a mathematical point, that has neither length, breadth, nor thickness. David Hume, speaking of theologians, has ingeniously observed, *that they have discovered the solution of the famous problem of Archimedes-- a point in the heavens, whence they move the world*.

27. Religion prostrates men before a being, who, without extension, is infinite, and fills all with his immensity; a being, all-powerful, who never executes his will; a being, sovereignly good, who creates only disquietudes; a being, the friend of order, and in whose government all is in confusion and disorder. What then, can we imagine, can be the God of theology?

28. To avoid all embarrassment, we are told, "that it is not necessary to know

what God is; that we must adore him; that we are not permitted to extend our views to his attributes." But, before we know that we must adore a God, must we not know certainly, that he exists? But, how can we assure ourselves, that he exists, if we never examine whether the various qualities, attributed to him, do really exist and agree in him? Indeed, to adore God, is to adore only the fictions of one's own imagination, or rather, it is to adore nothing.

29. In view of confounding things the more, theologians have not declared what their God is; they tell us only what he is not. By means of negations and abstractions, they think they have composed a real and perfect being. Mind is that, which is *not* body. An infinite being is a being, who is *not* finite. A perfect being is a being, who is *not* imperfect. Indeed, is there any one, who can form real ideas of such a mass of absence of ideas? That, which excludes all idea, can it be any thing but nothing?

To pretend, that the divine attributes are beyond the reach of human conception, is to grant, that God is not made for man. To assure us, that, in God, all is infinite, is to own that there can be nothing common to him and his creatures. If there be nothing common to God and his creatures, God is annihilated for man, or, at least, rendered useless to him. "God," they say, "has made man intelligent, but he has not made him omniscient;" hence it is inferred, that he has not been able to give him faculties sufficiently enlarged to know his divine essence. In this case, it is evident, that God has not been able nor willing to be known by his creatures. By what right then would God be angry with beings, who were naturally incapable of knowing the divine essence? God would be evidently the most unjust and capricious of tyrants, if he should punish an Atheist for not having known, what, by his nature, it was impossible he should know.

30. To the generality of men, nothing renders an argument more convincing than fear. It is therefore, that theologians assure us, *we must take the safest part*; that nothing is so criminal as incredulity; that God will punish without pity every one who has the temerity to doubt his existence; that his severity is just, since madness or perversity only can make us deny the existence of an enraged monarch, who without mercy avenges himself on Atheists. If we coolly examine these threatenings, we shall find, they always suppose the thing in question. They must first prove the existence of a God, before they assure us, it is safest to believe, and horrible to

doubt or deny his existence. They must then prove, that it is possible and consistent, that a just God cruelly punishes men for having been in a state of madness, that prevented their believing the existence of a being, whom their perverted reason could not conceive. In a word, they must prove, that an infinitely just God can infinitely punish the invincible and natural ignorance of man with respect to the divine nature. Do not theologians reason very strangely? They invent phantoms, they compose them of contradictions; they then assure us, it is safest not to doubt the existence of these phantoms they themselves have invented. According to this mode of reasoning, there is no absurdity, which it would not be more safe to believe, than not to believe.

All children are born Atheists; they have no idea of God. Are they then criminal on account of their ignorance? At what age must they begin to believe in God? It is, you say, at the age of reason. But at what time should this age commence? Besides, if the profoundest theologians lose themselves in the divine nature, which they do not presume to comprehend, what ideas must man have of him?

31. Men believe in God only upon the word of those, who have no more idea of him than themselves. Our nurses are our first theologians. They talk to children of God as if he were a scarecrow; they teach them from the earliest age to join their hands mechanically. Have nurses then more true ideas of God than the children whom they teach to pray?

32. Religion, like a family estate, passes, with its incumbrances, from parents to children. Few men in the world would have a God, had not pains been taken in infancy to give them one. Each would receive from his parents and teachers the God whom they received from theirs; but each, agreeably to his disposition, would arrange, modify, and paint him in his own manner.

33. The brain of man, especially in infancy, is like soft wax, fit to receive every impression that is made upon it. Education furnishes him with almost all his ideas at a time, when he is incapable of judging for himself. We believe we have received from nature, or have brought with us at birth, the true or false ideas, which, in a tender age, had been instilled into our minds; and this persuasion is one of the greatest sources of errors.

34. Prejudice contributes to cement in us the opinions of those who have been charged with our instruction. We believe them much more experienced than our-

selves; we suppose they are fully convinced of the things which they teach us; we
have the greatest confidence in them; by the care they have taken of us in infancy,
we judge them incapable of wishing to deceive us. These are the motives that make
us adopt a thousand errors, without other foundation than the hazardous authority
of those by whom we have been brought up. The prohibition likewise of reasoning
upon what they teach us, by no means lessens our confidence; but often contributes
to increase our respect for their opinions.

35. Divines act very wisely in teaching men their religious principles before
they are capable of distinguishing truth from falsehood, or their left hand from
their right. It would be as difficult to instill into the mind of a man, forty years old,
the extravagant notions that are given us of the divinity, as to eradicate them from
the mind of him who had imbibed them from infancy.

36. It is observed, that the wonders of nature are sufficient to lead us to the
existence of a God, and fully to convince us of this important truth. But how many
are there in the world who have the time, capacity, or disposition, necessary to contemplate Nature and meditate her progress? Men, for the most part, pay no regard
to it. The peasant is not struck with the beauty of the sun, which he sees every day.
The sailor is not surprised at the regular motion of the ocean; he will never draw
from it theological conclusions. The phenomena of nature prove the existence of a
God only to some prejudiced men, who have been early taught to behold the finger
of God in every thing whose mechanism could embarrass them. In the wonders
of nature, the unprejudiced philosopher sees nothing but the power of nature, the
permanent and various laws, the necessary effects of different combinations of matter infinitely diversified.

37. Is there any thing more surprising than the logic of these divines, who, instead of confessing their ignorance of natural causes, seek beyond nature, in imaginary regions, a cause much more unknown than that nature, of which they can
form at least some idea? To say, that God is the author of the phenomena of nature,
is it not to attribute them to an occult cause? What is God? What is a spirit? They
are causes of which we have no idea. O wise divines! Study nature and her laws;
and since you can there discover the action of natural causes, go not to those that
are supernatural, which, far from enlightening, will only darken your ideas, and
make it utterly impossible that you should understand yourselves.

38. Nature, you say, is totally inexplicable without a God. That is to say, to explain what you understand very little, you have need of a cause which you understand not at all. You think to elucidate what is obscure, by doubling the obscurity; to solve difficulties, by multiplying them. O enthusiastic philosophers! To prove the existence of a God, write complete treatises of botany; enter into a minute detail of the parts of the human body; launch forth into the sky, to contemplate the revolution of the stars; then return to the earth to admire the course of waters; behold with transport the butterflies, the insects, the polypi, and the organized atoms, in which you think you discern the greatness of your God. All these things will not prove the existence of God; they will prove only, that you have not just ideas of the immense variety of matter, and of the effects, producible by its infinitely diversified combinations, that constitute the universe. They will prove only your ignorance of nature; that you have no idea of her powers, when you judge her incapable of producing a multitude of forms and beings, of which your eyes, even with the assistance of microscopes, never discern but the smallest part. In a word, they will prove, that, for want of knowing sensible agents, or those possible to know, you find it shorter to have recourse to a word, expressing an inconceivable agent.

39. We are gravely and repeatedly told, that, *there is no effect without a cause*; that, *the world did not make itself*. But the universe is a cause, it is not an effect; it is not a work; it has not been made, because it is impossible that it should have been made. The world has always been; its existence is necessary; it is its own cause. Nature, whose essence is visibly to act and produce, requires not, to discharge her functions, an invisible mover, much more unknown than herself. Matter moves by its own energy, by a necessary consequence of its heterogeneity. The diversity of motion, or modes of mutual action, constitutes alone the diversity of matter. We distinguish beings from one another only by the different impressions or motions which they communicate to our organs.

40. You see, that all is action in nature, and yet pretend that nature, by itself, is dead and without power. You imagine, that this all, essentially acting, needs a mover! What then is this mover? It is a spirit; a being absolutely incomprehensible and contradictory. Acknowledge then, that matter acts of itself, and cease to reason of your spiritual mover, who has nothing that is requisite to put it in action. Return from your useless excursions; enter again into a real world; keep to *second causes*,

and leave to divines their *first cause*, of which nature has no need, to produce all the effects you observe in the world.

41. It can be only by the diversity of impressions and effects, which bodies make upon us, that we feel them; that we have perceptions and ideas of them; that we distinguish one from another; that we assign them properties. Now, to see or feel an object, the object must act upon our organs; this object cannot act upon us, without exciting some motion in us; it cannot excite motion in us, if it be not in motion itself. At the instant I see an object, my eyes are struck by it; I can have no conception of light and vision, without motion, communicated to my eye, from the luminous, extended, coloured body. At the instant I smell something, my sense is irritated, or put in motion, by the parts that exhale from the odoriferous body. At the moment I hear a sound, the tympanum of my ear is struck by the air, put in motion by a sonorous body, which would not act if it were not in motion itself. Whence it evidently follows, that, without motion, I can neither feel, see, distinguish, compare, judge, nor occupy my thoughts upon any subject whatever.

We are taught, that *the essence of a thing is that from which all its properties flow*. Now, it is evident, that all the properties of bodies, of which we have ideas, are owing to motion, which alone informs us of their existence, and gives us the first conceptions of them. I cannot be informed of my own existence but by the motions I experience in myself. I am therefore forced to conclude, that motion is as essential to matter as extension, and that matter cannot be conceived without it.

Should any person deny, that motion is essential and necessary to matter; they cannot, at least, help acknowledging that bodies, which seem dead and inert, produce motion of themselves, when placed in a fit situation to act upon one another. For instance; phosphorus, when exposed to the air, immediately takes fire. Meal and water, when mixed, ferment. Thus dead matter begets motion of itself. Matter has then the power of self-motion; and nature, to act, has no need of a mover, whose pretended essence would hinder him from acting.

42. Whence comes man? What is his origin? Did the first man spring, ready formed, from the dust of the earth? Man appears, like all other beings, a production of nature. Whence came the first stones, the first trees, the first lions, the first elephants, the first ants, the first acorns? We are incessantly told to acknowledge and revere the hand of God, of an infinitely wise, intelligent and powerful maker, in

so wonderful a work as the human machine. I readily confess, that the human machine appears to me surprising. But as man exists in nature, I am not authorized to say that his formation, is above the power of nature. But I can much less conceive of this formation, when to explain it, I am told, that a pure spirit, who has neither eyes, feet, hands, head, lungs, mouth nor breath, made man by taking a little clay, and breathing upon it.

We laugh at the savage inhabitants of Paraguay, for calling themselves the descendants of the moon. The divines of Europe call themselves the descendants, or the creation, of a pure spirit. Is this pretension any more rational? Man is intelligent; thence it is inferred, that he can be the work only of an intelligent being, and not of a nature, which is void of intelligence. Although nothing is more rare, than to see man make use of this intelligence, of which he seems so proud, I will grant that he is intelligent, that his wants develop this faculty, that society especially contributes to cultivate it. But I see nothing in the human machine, and in the intelligence with which it is endued, that announces very precisely the infinite intelligence of the maker to whom it is ascribed. I see that this admirable machine is liable to be deranged; I see, that his wonderful intelligence is then disordered, and sometimes totally disappears; I infer, that human intelligence depends upon a certain disposition of the material organs of the body, and that we cannot infer the intelligence of God, any more from the intelligence of man, than from his materiality. All that we can infer from it, is, that God is material. The intelligence of man no more proves the intelligence of God, than the malice of man proves the malice of that God, who is the pretended maker of man. In spite of all the arguments of divines, God will always be a cause contradicted by its effects, or of which it is impossible to judge by its works. We shall always see evil, imperfection and folly result from such a cause, that is said to be full of goodness, perfection and wisdom.

43. "What?" you will say, "is intelligent man, is the universe, and all it contains, the effect of *chance*?" No; I repeat it, *the universe is not an effect*; it is the cause of all effects; every being it contains is the necessary effect of this cause, which sometimes shews us its manner of acting, but generally conceals its operations. Men use the word *chance* to hide their ignorance of true causes, which, though not understood, act not less according to certain laws. There is no effect without a cause. Nature is a word, used to denote the immense assemblage of beings, various matter, infinite

combinations, and diversified motions, that we behold. All bodies, organized or unorganized, are necessary effects of certain causes. Nothing in nature can happen by chance. Every thing is subject to fixed laws. These laws are only the necessary connection of certain effects with their causes. One atom of matter cannot meet another *by chance*; this meeting is the effect of permanent laws, which cause every being necessarily to act as it does, and hinder it from acting otherwise, in given circumstances. To talk of the *fortuitous concourse of atoms*, or to attribute some effects to chance, is merely saying that we are ignorant of the laws, by which bodies act, meet, combine, or separate.

Those, who are unacquainted with nature, the properties of beings, and the effects which must necessarily result from the concurrence of certain causes, think, that every thing takes place by chance. It is not chance, that has placed the sun in the centre of our planetary system; it is by its own essence, that the substance, of which it is composed, must occupy that place, and thence be diffused.

44. The worshippers of a God find, in the order of the universe, an invincible proof of the existence of an intelligent and wise being, who governs it. But this order is nothing but a series of movements necessarily produced by causes or circumstances, which are sometimes favourable, and sometimes hurtful to us: we approve of some, and complain of others.

Nature uniformly follows the same round; that is, the same causes produce the same effects, as long as their action is not disturbed by other causes, which force them to produce different effects. When the operation of causes, whose effects we experience, is interrupted by causes, which, though unknown, are not the less natural and necessary, we are confounded; we cry out, *a miracle!* and attribute it to a cause much more unknown, than any of those acting before our eyes.

The universe is always in order. It cannot be in disorder. It is our machine, that suffers, when we complain of disorder. The bodies, causes, and beings, which this world contains, necessarily act in the manner in which we see them act, whether we approve or disapprove of their effects. Earthquakes, volcanoes, inundations, pestilences, and famines are effects as necessary, or as much in the order of nature, as the fall of heavy bodies, the courses of rivers, the periodical motions of the seas, the blowing of the winds, the fruitful rains, and the favourable effects, for which men praise God, and thank him for his goodness.

To be astonished that a certain order reigns in the world, is to be surprised that the same causes constantly produce the same effects. To be shocked at disorder, is to forget, that when things change, or are interrupted in their actions, the effects can no longer be the same. To wonder at the order of nature, is to wonder that any thing can exist; it is to be surprised at any one's own existence. What is order to one being, is disorder to another. All wicked beings find that every thing is in order, when they can with impunity put every thing in disorder. They find, on the contrary, that every thing is in disorder, when they are disturbed in the exercise of their wickedness.

45. Upon supposition that God is the author and mover of nature, there could be no disorder with respect to him. Would not all the causes, that he should have made, necessarily act according to the properties, essences, and impulses given them? If God should change the ordinary course of nature, he would not be immutable. If the order of the universe, in which man thinks he sees the most convincing proof of the existence, intelligence, power and goodness of God, should happen to contradict itself, one might suspect his existence, or, at least, accuse him of inconstancy, impotence, want of foresight and wisdom in the arrangement of things; one would have a right to accuse him of an oversight in the choice of the agents and instruments, which he makes, prepares, and puts in action. In short, if the order of nature proves the power and intelligence of the Deity, disorder must prove his weakness, instability, and irrationality.

You say, that God is omnipresent, that he fills the universe with his immensity, that nothing is done without him, that matter could not act without his agency. But in this case, you admit, that your God is the author of disorder, that it is he who deranges nature, that he is the father of confusion, that he is in man, and moves him at the moment he sins. If God is every where, he is in me, he acts with me, he is deceived with me, he offends God with me, and combats with me the existence of God! O theologians! you never understand yourselves, when you speak of God.

46. In order to have what we call intelligence, it is necessary to have ideas, thoughts, and wishes; to have ideas, thoughts, and wishes, it is necessary to have organs; to have organs, it is necessary to have a body; to act upon bodies, it is necessary to have a body; to experience disorder, it is necessary to be capable of suffering. Whence it evidently follows, that a pure spirit can neither be intelligent, nor

affected by what passes in the universe.

Divine intelligence, ideas, and views, have, you say, nothing common with those of men. Very well. How then can men judge, right or wrong, of these views; reason upon these ideas; or admire this intelligence? This would be to judge, admire, and adore that, of which we can have no ideas. To adore the profound views of divine wisdom, is it not to adore that, of which we cannot possibly judge? To admire these views, is it not to admire without knowing why? Admiration is always the daughter of ignorance. Men admire and adore only what they do not comprehend.

47. All those qualities, ascribed to God, are totally incompatible with a being, who, by his very essence, is void of all analogy with human beings. It is true, the divines imagine they extricate themselves from this difficulty, by exaggerating the human qualities, attributed to the Divinity; they enlarge them to infinity, where they cease to understand themselves. What results from this combination of man with God? A mere chimera, of which, if any thing be affirmed, the phantom, combined with so much pains, instantly vanishes.

Dante, in his poem upon *Paradise*, relates, that the Deity appeared to him under the figure of three circles, forming an iris, whose lively colours generated each other; but that, looking steadily upon the dazzling light, he saw only his own figure. While adoring God, it is himself, that man adores.

48. Ought not the least reflection suffice to prove, that God can have none of the human qualities, all ties, virtues, or perfections? Our virtues and perfections are consequences of the modifications of our passions. But has God passions as we have? Again: our good qualities consist in our dispositions towards the beings with whom we live in society. God, according to you, is an insulated being. God has no equals--no fellow-beings. God does not live in society. He wants the assistance of no one. He enjoys an unchangeable felicity. Admit then, according to your own principles, that God cannot have what we call virtues, and that man cannot be virtuous with respect to him.

49. Man, wrapped up in his own merit, imagines the human race to be the sole object of God in creating the universe. Upon what does he found this flattering opinion? We are told: that man is the only being endued with intelligence, which enables him to know the Deity, and to render him homage. We are assured, that

God made the world only for his own glory, and that it was necessary that the human species should come into this plan, that there might be some one to admire his works, and glorify him for them. But, according to these suppositions, has not God evidently missed his object? 1st. Man, according to yourselves, will always labour under the completest impossibility of knowing his God, and the most invincible ignorance of his divine essence. 2ndly. A being, who has no equal, cannot be susceptible of glory; for glory can result only from the comparison of one's own excellence with that of others. 3rdly. If God be infinitely happy, if he be self-sufficient, what need has he of the homage of his feeble creatures? 4thly. God, notwithstanding all his endeavours, is not glorified; but, on the contrary, all the religions in the world represent him as perpetually offended; their sole object is to reconcile sinful, ungrateful, rebellious man with his angry God.

50. If God be infinite, he has much less relation with man, than man with ants. Would the ants reason pertinently concerning the intentions, desires, and projects of the gardener? Could they justly imagine, that a park was planted for them alone, by an ostentatious monarch, and that the sole object of his goodness was to furnish them with a superb residence? But, according to theology, man is, with respect to God, far below what the vilest insect is to man. Thus, by theology itself, which is wholly devoted to the attributes and views of the Divinity, theology appears a complete folly.

51. We are told, that, in the formation of the universe, God's only object was the happiness of man. But, in a world made purposely for him, and governed by an omnipotent God, is man in reality very happy? Are his enjoyments durable? Are not his pleasures mixed with pains? Are many persons satisfied with their fate? Is not man continually the victim of physical and moral evils? Is not the human machine, which is represented as a master-piece of the Creator's skill, liable to derangement in a thousand ways? Should we be surprised at the workmanship of a mechanic, who should shew us a complex machine, ready to stop every moment, and which, in a short time, would break in pieces of itself?

52. The generous care, displayed by the Deity in providing for the wants, and watching over the happiness of his beloved creatures, is called *Providence*. But, when we open our eyes, we find that God provides nothing. Providence sleeps over the greater part of the inhabitants of this world. For a very small number of men

who are supposed to be happy, what an immense multitude groan under oppression, and languish in misery! Are not nations forced to deprive themselves of bread, to administer to the extravagances of a few gloomy tyrants, who are no happier than their oppressed slaves?

At the same time that our divines emphatically expatiate upon the goodness of Providence, while they exhort us to repose our confidence in her, do we not hear them, at the sight of unforeseen catastrophes, exclaim, that *Providence sports with the vain projects of man*, that she frustrates their designs, that she laughs at their efforts, that profound wisdom delights to bewilder the minds of mortals? But, shall we put confidence in a malignant Providence, who laughs at, and sports with mankind? How will one admire the unknown ways of a hidden wisdom, whose manner of acting is inexplicable? Judge of it by effects, you will say. We do; and find, that these effects are sometimes useful, and sometimes hurtful.

Men think they justify Providence, by saying, that, in this world, there is much more good than evil to every individual of mankind. Supposing the good, we enjoy from Providence, is to the evil, as a *hundred to ten*; will it not still follow, that, for a hundred degrees of goodness, Providence possesses ten of malignity; which is incompatible with the supposed perfection of the divine nature.

Almost all books are filled with the most flattering praises of Providence, whose attentive care is highly extolled. It would seem as if man, to live happily here below, needed not his own exertions. Yet, without his own labour, man could subsist hardly a day. To live, he is obliged to sweat, toil, hunt, fish, and labour without intermission. Without these second causes, the first cause, at least in most countries, would provide for none of our wants. In all parts of the globe, we see savage and civilized man in a perpetual struggle with Providence. He is necessitated to ward off the strokes directed against him by Providence, in hurricanes, tempests, frosts, hail-storms, inundations, droughts, and the various accidents, which so often render useless all his labours. In a word, we see man continually occupied in guarding against the ill offices of that Providence, which is supposed to be attentive to his happiness.

A bigot admired divine Providence for wisely ordering rivers to pass through those places, where men have built large cities. Is not this man's reasoning as rational, as that of many learned men, who incessantly talk of *final causes*, or who pretend that they clearly perceive the beneficent views of God in the formation of all things?

53. Do we see then, that Providence so very sensibly manifests herself in the preservation of those admirable works, which we attribute to her? If it is she, who governs the world, we find her as active in destroying, as in forming; in exterminating, as in producing. Does she not every moment destroy, by thousands, the very men, to whose preservation and welfare we suppose her continually attentive? Every moment she loses sight of her beloved creature. Sometimes she shakes his dwelling, sometimes she annihilates his harvests, sometimes she inundates his fields, sometimes she desolates them by a burning drought. She arms all nature against man. She arms man himself against his own species, and commonly terminates his existence in anguish. Is this then what is called preserving the universe?

If we could view, without prejudice, the equivocal conduct of Providence towards the human race and all sensible beings, we should find, that far from resembling a tender and careful mother, she resembles rather those unnatural mothers, who instantly forgetting the unfortunates of their licentious love, abandon their infants, as soon as they are born, and who, content with having borne them, expose them, helpless, to the caprice of fortune.

The Hottentots, in this respect are much wiser than other nations, who treat them as barbarians, and refuse to worship God; because, they say, *if he often does good, he often does evil*. Is not this manner of reasoning more just and conformable to experience, than that of many men, who are determined to see, in their God, nothing but goodness, wisdom, and foresight, and who refuse to see that the innumerable evils, of which this world is the theatre, must come from the same hand, which they kiss with delight?

54. Common sense teaches, that we cannot, and ought not, to judge of a cause, but by its effects. A cause can be reputed constantly good, only when it constantly produces good. A cause, which produces both good and evil, is sometimes good, and sometimes evil. But the logic of theology destroys all this. According to that, the phenomena of nature, or the effects we behold in this world, prove to us the existence of a cause infinitely good; and this cause is God. Although this world is full of evils; although disorder often reigns in it; although men incessantly repine at their hard fate; we must be convinced, that these effects are owing to a beneficent

and immutable cause; and many people believe it, or feign believe.

Every thing that passes in the world, proves to us, in the clearest manner, that it is not governed by an intelligent being. We can judge of the intelligence of a being only by the conformity of the means, which he employs to attain his proposed object. The object of God, is the happiness of a man. Yet, a like necessity governs the fate of all sensible beings, who are born only to suffer much, enjoy little, and die. The cup of man is filled with joy and bitterness; good is every where attended with evil; order gives place to disorder; generation is followed by destruction. If you say, that the designs of God are mysterious and that his ways are impenetrable; I answer, that, in this case, it is impossible to judge whether God be intelligent.

55. You pretend, that God is immutable! What then produces a continual instability in this world, which you make his empire? Is there a state, subject to more frequent and cruel revolutions, than that of this unknown monarch? How can we attribute to an immutable God, sufficiently powerful to give solidity to his works, a government, in which every thing is in continual vicissitude? If I imagine I see a God of uniform character in all the effects favourable to my species, what kind of a God can I see in their continual misfortunes? You tell me, it is our sins, which compel him to punish. I answer, that God, according to yourselves, is then not immutable, since the sins of men force him to change his conduct towards them. Can a being, who is sometimes provoked, and sometimes appeased, be constantly the same?

56. The universe can be only what it is; all sensible beings in it enjoy and suffer; that is, are moved sometimes in an agreeable, and sometimes in a disagreeable manner. These effects are necessary; they result necessarily from causes, which act only according to their properties. These effects necessarily please, or displease, by a consequence of nature. This same nature compels me to avoid, avert, and resist some things, and to seek, desire, and procure others. In a world, where every thing is necessary, a God, who remedies nothing, who leaves things to run in their necessary course,--is he any thing but destiny, or necessity personified? It is a deaf and useless God, who can effect no change in general laws, to which he is himself subject. Of what importance is the infinite power of a being, who will do but very little in my favour? Where is the infinite goodness of a being, indifferent to happiness? Of what service is the favour of a being, who, is able to do an infinite good,

does not do even a finite one?

57. When we ask, why so many miserable objects appear under the government of a good God, we are told, by way of consolation, that the present world is only a passage, designed to conduct man to a happier one. The divines assure us, that the earth we inhabit, is a state of trial. In short, they shut our mouths, by saying, that God could communicate to his creatures neither impossibility nor infinite happiness, which are reserved for himself alone. Can such answers be satisfactory? 1st. The existence of another life is guaranteed to us only by the imagination of man, who, by supposing it, have only realized the desire they have of surviving themselves, in order to enjoy hereafter a purer and more durable happiness. 2ndly. How can we conceive that a God, who knows every thing, and must be fully acquainted with the dispositions of his creatures, should want so many experiments, in order to be sure of their dispositions? 3rdly. According to the calculations of their chronologists, our earth has existed six or seven thousand years. During that time, nations have experienced calamities. History exhibits the human species at all times tormented and ravaged by tyrants, conquerors, and heroes; by wars, inundations, famines, plagues, etc. Are such long trials then likely to inspire us with very great confidence in the secret views of the Deity? Do such numerous and constant evils give a very exalted idea of the future state, his goodness is preparing for us? 4thly. If God is so kindly disposed, as he is asserted to be, without giving men infinite happiness, could he not at least have communicated the degree of happiness, of which finite beings are susceptible here below? To be happy, must we have an *infinite* or *divine* happiness? 5thly. If God could not make men happier than they are here below, what will become of the hope of a *paradise*, where it is pretended, that the elect will for ever enjoy ineffable bliss? If God neither could nor would avert evil from the earth, the only residence we can know, what reason have we to presume, that he can or will avert evil from another world, of which we have no idea? Epicurus observed: "either God would remove evil out of this world, and cannot; or he can, and will not; or he has neither the power nor will; or, lastly, he has both the power and will. If he has the will, and not the power, this shews weakness, which is contrary to the nature of God. If he has the power, and not the will, it is malignity; and this is no less contrary to his nature. If he is neither able nor willing, he is both impotent and malignant, and consequently cannot be God. If

he be both willing and able (which alone is consonant to the nature of God) whence comes evil, or why does he not prevent it?" Reflecting minds are still waiting for a reasonable solution of these difficulties; and our divines tell us, that they will be removed only in a future life.

58. We are told of a pretended *scale of beings*. It is supposed, that God has divided his creatures into different classes, in which each enjoys the degree of happiness, of which it is susceptible. According to this romantic arrangement, from the oyster to the celestial angels, all beings enjoy a happiness, which is suitable to their nature. Experience explicitly contradicts this sublime reverie. In this world, all sensible beings suffer and live in the midst of dangers. Man cannot walk without hurting, tormenting, or killing a multitude of sensible beings, which are in his way; while he himself is exposed, at every step, to a multitude of evils, foreseen or unforeseen, which may lead him to destruction. During the whole course of his life, he is exposed to pains; he is not sure, a moment, of his existence, to which he is so strongly attached, and which he regards as the greatest gift of the Divinity.

59. The world, it will be said, has all the perfection, of which it is susceptible: since it is not God who made it, it must have great qualities and great defects. But we answer, that, as the world must necessarily have great defects, it would have been more conformable to the nature of a good God, not to have created a world, which he could not make completely happy. If God was supremely happy, before the creation of the world, and could have continued to be supremely happy, without creating the world, why did he not remain at rest? Why must man suffer? Why must man exist? Of what importance is his existence to God? Nothing, or something? If man's existence is not useful or necessary to God, why did God make man? If man's existence is necessary to God's glory, he had need of man; he was deficient in something before man existed. We can pardon an unskilful workman for making an imperfect work; because he must work, well or ill, upon penalty of starving. This workman is excusable, but God is not. According to you, he is self-sufficient; if so, why does he make men? He has, you say, every thing requisite to make man happy. Why then does he not do it? Confess, that your God has more malice than goodness, unless you admit, that God, was necessitated to do what he has done, without being able to do it otherwise. Yet, you assure us, that God is free. You say also, that he is immutable, although it was in *Time* that he began and ceased to

exercise his power, like the inconstant beings of this world. O theologians! Vain are your efforts to free your God from defects. This perfect God has always some human imperfections.

60. "Is not God master of his favours? Can he not give them? Can he not take them away? It does not belong to his creatures to require reasons for his conduct. He can dispose of the works of his own hands as he pleases. Absolute sovereign of mortals, he distributes happiness or misery, according to his good pleasure." Such are the solutions given by theologians to console us for the evils which God inflicts upon us. We reply, that a God, who is infinitely good, cannot be *master of his favours*, but would by his nature be obliged to bestow them upon his creatures; that a being, truly beneficent, cannot refrain from doing good; that a being, truly generous, does not take back what he has given; and that every man, who does so, dispenses with gratitude, and has no right to complain of finding ungrateful men.

How can the odd and capricious conduct, which theologians ascribe to God, be reconciled with religion, which supposes a covenant, or mutual engagements between God and men? If God owes nothing to his creatures, they, on their part, can owe nothing to their God. All religion is founded upon the happiness that men think they have a right to expect from the Deity, who is supposed to say to them: *Love me, adore me, obey me: and I will make you happy*. Men, on their part, say to him: *Make us happy, be faithful to your promises, and we will love you, we will adore you, and obey your laws*. By neglecting the happiness of his creatures, distributing his favours according to his caprice, and retracting his gifts, does not God break the covenant, which serves as the basis of all religion? Cicero has justly observed, that *if God is not agreeable to man, he cannot be his God*. Goodness constitutes deity; this goodness can be manifested to man only by the blessings he enjoys; as soon as he is unhappy, this goodness disappears, and with it the divinity. An infinite goodness can be neither limited, partial, nor exclusive. If God be infinitely good, he owes happiness to all his creatures. The unhappiness of a single being would suffice to annihilate unbounded goodness. Under an infinitely good and powerful God, is it possible to conceive that a single man should suffer? One animal, or mite, that suffers, furnishes invincible arguments against divine providence and its infinite goodness.

61. According to theology, the afflictions and evils of this life are chastisements, which guilty men incur from the hand of God. But why are men guilty? If

God is omnipotent, does it cost him more to say: "Let every thing in the world be in order; let all my subjects be good, innocent, and fortunate," than to say: "Let every thing exist"? Was it more difficult for this God to do his work well, than badly? Religion tells us of a hell; that is, a frightful abode, where, notwithstanding his goodness, God reserves infinite torments for the majority of men. Thus after having rendered mortals very unhappy in this world, religion tells them, that God can render them still more unhappy in another! The theologian gets over this, by saying, that the goodness of God will then give place to his justice. But a goodness, which gives place to the most terrible cruelty, is not an infinite goodness. Besides, can a God, who, after having been infinitely good, becomes infinitely bad, be regarded as an immutable being? Can we discern the shadow of clemency or goodness, in a God filled with implacable fury?

62. Divine justice, as stated by our divines, is undoubtedly a quality very proper to cherish in us the love of the Divinity. According to the ideas of modern theology, it is evident, that God has created the majority of men, with the sole view of putting them in a fair way to incur eternal punishment. Would it not have been more conformable to goodness, reason, and equity, to have created only stones or plants, and not to have created sensible beings; than to have formed men, whose conduct in this world might subject them to endless punishment in the other? A God perfidious and malicious enough to create a single man, and then to abandon him to the danger of being damned, cannot be regarded as a perfect being; but as an unreasonable, unjust, and ill-natured. Very far from composing a perfect God, theologians have formed the most imperfect of beings. According to theological notions, God would resemble a tyrant, who, having put out the eyes of the greater part of his slaves, should shut them up in a dungeon, where, for his amusement, he would, incognito, observe their conduct through a trap-door, in order to punish with rigour all those, who, while walking about, should hit against each other; but who would magnificently reward the few whom he had not deprived of sight, in avoiding to run against their comrades. Such are the ideas, which the dogma of gratuitous predestination gives us of the divinity!

Although men are continually repeating that their God is infinitely good; yet it is evident, that in reality, they can believe nothing of the kind. How can we love what we do not know? How can we love a being, whose character is only fit to throw us into inquietude and trouble? How can we love a being, of whom all that is said tends to render him an object of utter detestation?

63. Many people make a subtle distinction between true religion and superstition. They say, that the latter is only a base and inordinate fear of the Deity; but that the truly religious man has confidence in his God, and loves him sincerely; whereas, the superstitious man sees in him only an enemy, has no confidence in him, and represents him to himself as a distrustful, cruel tyrant, sparing of his benefits, lavish of his chastisements. But, in reality, does not all religion give us the same ideas of God? At the same time that we are told, that God is infinitely good, are we not also told, that he is very easily provoked, that he grants his favours to a few people only, and that he furiously chastises those, to whom he has not been pleased to grant favours?

64. If we take our ideas of God from the nature of things, where we find a mixture of good and evil, this God, just like the good and evil of which we experience, must naturally appear capricious, inconstant, sometimes good, and sometimes malevolent; and therefore, instead of exciting our love, must generate distrust, fear, and uncertainty. There is then no real difference between natural religion, and the most gloomy and servile superstition. If the theist sees God only in a favourable light; the bigot views him in the most hideous light. The folly of the one is cheerful, that of the other is melancholy; but both are equally delirious.

65. If I draw my ideas of God from theology, he appears to inspire aversion. Devotees, who tell us, that they sincerely love their God, are either liars or fools, who see their God only in profile. It is impossible to love a being, the very idea of whom strikes us with terror, and whose judgments make us tremble. How can we, without being alarmed, look upon a God, who is reputed to be barbarous enough to damn us? Let not divines talk to us of a filial, or respectful fear, mixed with love, which men ought to have for their God. A son can by no means love his father, when he knows him to be cruel enough to inflict upon him studied torments for the least faults he may commit. No man upon earth can have the least spark of love for a God, who reserves chastisements, infinite in duration and violence, for ninety-nine hundredths of his children.

66. The inventors of the dogma of eternal hell-torments have made of that God, whom they call so good, the most detestable of beings. Cruelty in men is the

last act of wickedness. Every sensible mind must revolt at the bare recital of the torments, inflicted on the greatest criminal; but cruelty is much more apt to excite indignation, when void of motives. The most sanguinary tyrants, the Caligulas, the Neros, the Domitians, had, at least, some motives for tormenting their victims. These motives were, either their own safety, or the fury of revenge, or the design of frightening by terrible examples, or perhaps the vanity of making a display of their power, and the desire of satisfying a barbarous curiosity. Can a God have any of these motives? In tormenting the victims of his wrath, he would punish beings, who could neither endanger his immoveable power, nor disturb his unchangeable felicity. On the other hand, the punishments of the other life would be useless to the living, who cannot be witnesses of them. These punishments would be useless to the damned, since in hell there is no longer room for conversion, and the time of mercy is past. Whence it follows, that God, in the exercise of his eternal vengeance, could have no other end than to amuse himself, and insult the weakness of his creatures. I appeal to the whole human race;--is there a man who feels cruel enough coolly to torment, I do not say his fellow-creature, but any sensible being whatever, without emolument, without profit, without curiosity, without having any thing to fear? Confess then, O theologians, that, even according to your own principles, your God is infinitely more malevolent than the worst of men.

Perhaps you will say, that infinite offences deserve infinite punishments. I answer, that we cannot offend a God, whose happiness is infinite; that the offences of finite beings cannot be infinite; that a God, who is unwilling to be offended, cannot consent that the offences of his creatures should be eternal; that a God, infinitely good, can neither be infinitely cruel, nor grant his creatures an infinite duration, solely for the pleasure of eternal torments.

Nothing but the most savage barbarity, the most egregious roguery, or the blindest ambition could have imagined the doctrine of eternal punishments. If there is a God, whom we can offend or blaspheme, there are not upon earth greater blasphemers than those, who dare to say, that this same God is a tyrant, perverse enough to delight, during eternity, in the useless torments of his feeble creatures.

67. To pretend, that God can be offended at the actions of men, is to annihilate all the ideas, which divines endeavour to give us, in other respects, of this being. To say, that man can trouble the order of the universe; that he can kindle the thunder

in the hands of his God; that he can defeat his projects, is to say, that man is stronger than his God, that he is the arbiter of his will, that it depends upon him to change his goodness into cruelty. Theology continually pulls down, with one hand, what it erects with the other. If all religion is founded upon a God, who is provoked and appeased, all religion is founded on a palpable contradiction.

All religions agree in exalting the wisdom and infinite power of the Deity. But no sooner do they display his conduct, than we see nothing but imprudence, want of foresight, weakness and folly. God, it is said, created the world for himself; and yet, hitherto, he has never been able to make himself suitably honoured by it. God created men in order to have, in his dominions, subjects to render him their homage; and yet, we see men in continual revolt against him.

68. They incessantly extol the divine perfections; and when we demand proofs of them, they point to his works, in which, they assure us, these perfections are written in indelible characters. All these works are, however, imperfect and perishable. Man, who is ever regarded as the most marvellous work, as the masterpiece of the Deity, is full of imperfections, which render him disagreeable to the eyes of the almighty Being, who formed him. This surprising work often becomes so revolting and odious to its author, that he is obliged to throw it into the fire. But, if the fairest of God's works is imperfect, how can we judge of the divine perfections? Can a work, with which the author himself is so little pleased, induce us to admire the ability of its Maker? Man, considered in a physical sense, is subject to a thousand infirmities, to numberless evils, and to death. Man, considered in a moral sense, is full of faults; yet we are unceasingly told, that he is the most beautiful work of the most perfect of beings.

69. In creating beings more perfect than men, it appears, that heretofore God has not better succeeded, nor given stronger proofs of his perfection. Do we not see, in many religions, that angels, have even attempted to dethrone him? God proposed the happiness of angels and men; yet, he has never been able to render happy either angels or men;--the pride, malice, sins, and imperfections of the creatures have always opposed the will of the perfect Creator.

70. All religion is obviously founded upon this principle, that *God does what he can, and man what he will*. Every system of religion presents to us an unequal combat between the Deity on one part, and his creatures on the other, in which the former

never comes off to his honour. Notwithstanding his omnipotence, he cannot succeed in rendering the works of his hands such as he would have them. To complete the absurdity, there is a religion, which pretends, that God himself has died to redeem mankind; and yet, men are not farther from any thing, than they are from what God would have them.

71. Nothing is more extravagant, than the part, theology makes the Divinity act in every country. Did he really exist, we should see in him the most capricious, and senseless being. We should be compelled to believe, that God made the world only to be the theatre of his disgraceful wars with his creatures; that he created angels, men, and demons, only to make adversaries, against whom he might exercise his power. He renders men free to offend him, malicious enough to defeat his projects, too obstinate to submit; and all this merely for the pleasure of being angry, appeased, reconciled, and of repairing the disorder they have made. Had the Deity at once formed his creatures such as he would have them, what pains would he not have spared himself, or, at least, from what embarrassments would he not have relieved his theologians!

Every religion represents God as busy only in doing himself evil. He resembles those empirics, who inflict upon themselves wounds, to have an opportunity of exhibiting to the public the efficacy of their ointment. But we see not, that the Deity has hitherto been able radically to cure himself of the evil, which he suffers from man.

72. God is the author of all; and yet, we are assured that evil does not come from God. Whence then does it come? From man. But, who made man? God. Evil then comes from God. If he had not made man as he is, moral evil or sin would not have existed in the world. The perversity of man is therefore chargeable to God. If man has power to do evil, or to offend God, we are forced to infer, that God chooses to be offended; that God, who made man, has resolved that man shall do evil; otherwise man would be an effect contrary to the cause, from which he derives his being.

73. Man ascribes to God the faculty of foreseeing, or knowing beforehand whatever will happen; but this prescience seldom turns to his glory, nor protects him from the lawful reproaches of man. If God foreknows the future, must he not have foreseen the fall of his creatures? If he resolved in his decrees to permit this

fall, it is undoubtedly because it was his will that this fall should take place, otherwise it could not have happened. If God's foreknowledge of the sins of his creatures had been necessary or forced, one might suppose, that he has been constrained by his justice to punish the guilty; but, enjoying the faculty of foreseeing, and the power of predetermining every thing, did it not depend upon God not to impose upon himself cruel laws, or, at least, could he not dispense with creating beings, whom he might be under the necessity of punishing, and rendering unhappy by a subsequent decree? Of what consequence is it, whether God has destined men to happiness or misery by an anterior decree, an effect of his prescience, or by a posterior decree, an effect of his justice? Does the arrangement of his decrees alter the fate of the unhappy? Would they not have the same right to complain of a God, who, being able to omit their creation, has notwithstanding created them, although he plainly foresaw that his justice would oblige him, sooner or later, to punish them?

74. "Man," you say, "when he came from the hand of God, was pure, innocent, and good; but his nature has been corrupted, as a punishment for sin." If man, when just out of the hands of his God, could sin, his nature was imperfect. Why did God suffer him to sin, and his nature to be corrupted? Why did God permit him to be seduced, well knowing that he was too feeble to resist temptation? Why did God create *satan*, an evil spirit, a tempter? Why did not God, who wishes so much good to the human race, annihilate once for all so many evil genii, who are naturally enemies of our happiness; or rather, why did God create evil spirits, whose victories and fatal influence over mankind, he must have foreseen? In fine, by what strange fatality in all religions of the world, has the evil principle such a decided advantage over the good principle, or the divinity?

75. There is related an instance of simplicity, which does honour to the heart of an Italian monk. One day, while preaching, this pious man thought he must announce to his audience, that he had, thank heaven, at last discovered, by dint of meditation, a sure way of rendering all men happy. "The devil," said he, "tempts men only to have in hell companions of his misery. Let us therefore apply to the Pope, who has the keys of heaven and hell; let us prevail upon him to pray to God, at the head of the whole church, to consent to a reconciliation with the devil, to restore him to favour, to reinstate him in his former rank, which cannot fail to put an end to his malicious projects against mankind." Perhaps the honest monk did

not see, that the devil is at least as useful as God to the ministers of religion. They have too much interest in their dissensions, to be instrumental in an accommodation between two enemies, upon whose combats their own existence and revenues depend. Let men cease to be tempted and to sin, and the ministry of priests will be useless. Manicheism is evidently the hinge of every religion; but unhappily, the devil, invented to clear the deity from the suspicion of malice, proves to us, every moment, the impotence or unskilfulness of his celestial adversary.

76. The nature of man, it is said, was necessarily liable to corruption. God could not communicate to him *impeccability*, which is an inalienable attribute of his divine perfection. But if God could not make man impeccable, why did he give himself the pains to make man, whose nature must necessarily be corrupted, and who must consequently offend God? On the other hand, if God himself could not make human nature impeccable, by what right does he punish men for not being impeccable? It can be only by the right of the strongest; but the right of the strongest is called violence, and violence cannot be compatible with the justest of beings. God would be supremely unjust, should he punish men for not sharing with him his divine perfections, or for not being able to be gods like him.

Could not God, at least, have communicated to all men that kind of perfection, of which their nature is susceptible? If some men are good, or render themselves agreeable to their God, why has not that God done the same favour, or given the same dispositions to all beings of our species? Why does the number of the wicked so much exceed the number of the good? Why, for one friend, has God ten thousand enemies, in a world, which it depended entirely upon him to people with honest men? If it be true, that, in heaven, God designs to form a court of saints, of elect, or of men who shall have lived upon earth conformably to his views, would he not have had a more numerous, brilliant, and honourable assembly, had he composed it of all men, to whom, in creating them, he could grant the degree of goodness, necessary to attain eternal happiness? Finally, would it not have been shorter not to have made man, than to have created him a being full of faults, rebellious to his creator, perpetually exposed to cause his own destruction by a fatal abuse of his liberty?

Instead of creating men, a perfect God ought to have created only angels very docile and submissive. Angels, it is said, are free; some have sinned; but, at any rate, all have not abused their liberty by revolting against their master. Could not God have created only angels of the good kind? If God has created angels, who have not sinned, could he not have created impeccable men, or men who should never abuse their liberty? If the elect are incapable of sinning in heaven, could not God have made impeccable men upon earth?

77. Divines never fail to persuade us, that the enormous distance which separates God and man, necessarily renders the conduct of God a mystery to us, and that we have no right to interrogate our master. Is this answer satisfactory? Since my eternal happiness is at stake, have I not a right to examine the conduct of God himself? It is only in hope of happiness that men submit to the authority of a God. A despot, to whom men submit only through fear, a master, whom they cannot interrogate, a sovereign totally inaccessible, can never merit the homage of intelligent beings. If the conduct of God is a mystery, it is not made for us. Man can neither adore, admire, respect, nor imitate conduct, in which every thing is inconceivable, or, of which he can often form only revolting ideas; unless it is pretended, that we ought to adore every thing of which we are forced to be ignorant, and that every thing, which we do not know, becomes for that reason an object of admiration. Divines! You never cease telling us, that the designs of God are impenetrable; that *his ways are not our ways, nor his thoughts our thoughts*; that it is absurd to complain of his administration, of the motives and springs of which we are totally ignorant; that it is presumption to tax his judgments with injustice, because we cannot comprehend them. But when you speak in this strain, do you not perceive, that you destroy with your own hands all your profound systems, whose only end is to explain to us the ways of the divinity, which, you say, are impenetrable? Have you penetrated his judgments, his ways, his designs? You dare not assert it, and though you reason about them without end, you do not comprehend them any more than we do. If, by chance, you know the plan of God, which you wish us to admire, while most people find it so little worthy of a just, good, intelligent, and reasonable being, no longer say, this plan is impenetrable. If you are as ignorant of it as we are, have some indulgence for those who ingenuously confess, they comprehend nothing in it, or that they see in it nothing divine. Cease to persecute for opinions, of which you understand nothing yourselves; cease to defame each other for dreams and conjectures, which every thing seems to contradict. Talk to us of things intelligible

and really useful to men; and no longer talk to us of the impenetrable ways of God, about which you only stammer and contradict yourselves.

By continually speaking of the immense depths of divine wisdom, forbidding us to sound them, saying it is insolence to cite God before the tribunal of our feeble reason, making it a crime to judge our master, divines teach us nothing but the embarrassment they are in, when it is required to account for the conduct of a God, whose conduct they think marvellous only because they are utterly incapable of comprehending it themselves.

78. Physical evil is commonly regarded as a punishment for sin. Diseases, famines, wars, earthquakes, are means which God uses to chastise wicked men. Thus, they make no scruple of attributing these evils to the severity of a just and good God. But, do not these scourges fall indiscriminately upon the good and bad, upon the impious and devout, upon the innocent and guilty? How, in this proceeding, would they have us admire the justice and goodness of a being, the idea of whom seems comforting to so many wretches, whose brain must undoubtedly be disordered by their misfortunes, since they forget, that their God is the arbiter, the sole disposer of the events of this world. This being the case, ought they not to impute their sufferings to him, into whose arms they fly for comfort? Unfortunate father! Thou consolest thyself in the bosom of Providence, for the loss of a dear child, or beloved wife, who made thy happiness. Alas! Dost thou not see, that thy God has killed them? Thy God has rendered thee miserable, and thou desirest thy God to comfort thee for the dreadful afflictions he has sent thee!

The chimerical or supernatural notions of theology have so succeeded in destroying, in the minds of men, the most simple, dear, and natural ideas, that the devout, unable to accuse God of malice, accustom themselves to regard the several strokes of fate as indubitable proofs of celestial goodness. When in affliction, they are ordered to believe that God loves them, that God visits them, that God wishes to try them. Thus religion has attained the art of converting evil into good! A profane person said with reason-- *If God Almighty thus treats those whom he loves, I earnestly beseech him never to think of me*.

Men must have received very gloomy and cruel ideas of their God, who is called so good, to believe that the most dreadful calamities and piercing afflictions are marks of his favour! Would an evil genius, a demon, be more ingenious in tormenting his enemies, than the God of goodness sometimes is, who so often exercises his severity upon his dearest friends?

79. What shall we say of a father, who, we are assured, watches without intermission over the preservation and happiness of his weak and short-sighted children, and who yet leaves them at liberty to wander at random among rocks, precipices, and waters; who rarely hinders them from following their inordinate appetites; who permits them to handle, without precaution, murderous arms, at the risk of their life? What should we think of the same father, if, instead of imputing to himself the evil that happens to his poor children, he should punish them for their wanderings in the most cruel manner? We should say, with reason, that this father is a madman, who unites injustice to folly. A God, who punishes faults, which he could have prevented, is a being deficient in wisdom, goodness, and equity. A foreseeing God would prevent evil, and thereby avoid having to punish it. A good God would not punish weaknesses, which he knew to be inherent in human nature. A just God, if he made man, would not punish him for not being made strong enough to resist his desires. *To punish weakness is the most unjust tyranny.* Is it not calumniating a just God, to say, that he punishes men for their faults, even in the present life? How could he punish beings, whom it belonged to him alone to reform, and who, while they have not *grace*, cannot act otherwise than they do?

According to the principles of theologians themselves, man, in his present state of corruption, can do nothing but evil, since, without divine grace, he is never able to do good. Now, if the nature of man, left to itself, or destitute of divine aid, necessarily determines him to evil, or renders him incapable of good, what becomes of the free-will of man? According to such principles, man can neither merit nor demerit. By rewarding man for the good he does, God would only reward himself; by punishing man for the evil he does, God would punish him for not giving him grace, without which he could not possibly do better.

80. Theologians repeatedly tell us, that man is free, while all their principles conspire to destroy his liberty. By endeavouring to justify the Divinity, they in reality accuse him of the blackest injustice. They suppose, that without grace, man is necessitated to do evil. They affirm, that God will punish him, because God has not given him grace to do good!

Little reflection will suffice to convince us, that man is necessitated in all his actions, that his free will is a chimera, even in the system of theologians. Does it depend upon man to be born of such or such parents? Does it depend upon man to imbibe or not to imbibe the opinions of his parents or instructors? If I had been born of idolatrous or Mahometan parents, would it have depended upon me to become a Christian? Yet, divines gravely assure us, that a just God will damn without pity all those, to whom he has not given grace to know the Christian religion!

Man's birth is wholly independent of his choice. He is not asked whether he is willing, or not, to come into the world. Nature does not consult him upon the country and parents she gives him. His acquired ideas, his opinions, his notions true or false, are necessary fruits of the education which he has received, and of which he has not been the director. His passions and desires are necessary consequences of the temperament given him by nature. During his whole life, his volitions and actions are determined by his connections, habits, occupations, pleasures, and conversations; by the thoughts, that are involuntarily presented to his mind; in a word, by a multitude of events and accidents, which it is out of his power to foresee or prevent. Incapable of looking into futurity, he knows not what he will do. From the instant of his birth to that of his death, he is never free. You will say, that he wills, deliberates, chooses, determines; and you will hence conclude, that his actions are free. It is true, that man wills, but he is not master of his will or his desires; he can desire and will only what he judges advantageous to himself; he can neither love pain, nor detest pleasure. It will be said, that he sometimes prefers pain to pleasure; but then he prefers a momentary pain with a view of procuring a greater and more durable pleasure. In this case, the prospect of a greater good necessarily determines him to forego a less considerable good.

The lover does not give his mistress the features which captivate him; he is not then master of loving, or not loving the object of his tenderness; he is not master of his imagination or temperament. Whence it evidently follows, that man is not master of his volitions and desires. "But man," you will say, "can resist his desires; therefore he is free." Man resists his desires, when the motives, which divert him from an object, are stronger than those, which incline him towards it; but then his resistance is necessary. A man, whose fear of dishonour or punishment is greater than his love of money, necessarily resists the desire of stealing.

"Are we not free, when we deliberate?" But, are we masters of knowing or not knowing, of being in doubt or certainty? Deliberation is a necessary effect of our uncertainty respecting the consequences of our actions. When we are sure, or think we are sure, of these consequences, we necessarily decide, and we then act necessarily according to our true or false judgment. Our judgments, true or false, are not free; they are necessarily determined by the ideas, we have received, or which our minds have formed.

Man is not free in his choice; he is evidently necessitated to choose what he judges most useful and agreeable. Neither is he free, when he suspends his choice; he is forced to suspend it until he knows, or thinks he knows, the qualities of the objects presented to him, or, until he has weighed the consequences of his actions. "Man," you will say, "often decides in favour of actions, which he knows must be detrimental to himself; man sometimes kills himself; therefore he is free." I deny it. Is man master of reasoning well or ill? Do not his reason and wisdom depend upon the opinions he has formed, or upon the conformation of his machine? As neither one nor the other depends upon his will, they are no proof of liberty. "If I lay a wager, that I shall do, or not do a thing, am I not free? Does it not depend upon me to do it or not?" No, I answer; the desire of winning the wager will necessarily determine you to do, or not to do the thing in question. "But, supposing I consent to lose the wager?" Then the desire of proving to me, that you are free, will have become a stronger motive than the desire of winning the wager; and this motive will have necessarily determined you to do, or not to do, the thing in question.

"But," you will say, "I feel free." This is an illusion, that may be compared to that of the fly in the fable, who, lighting upon the pole of a heavy carriage, applauded himself for directing its course. Man, who thinks himself free, is a fly, who imagines he has power to move the universe, while he is himself unknowingly carried along by it.

The inward persuasion that we are free to do, or not to do a thing, is but a mere illusion. If we trace the true principle of our actions, we shall find, that they are always necessary consequences of our volitions and desires, which are never in our power. You think yourself free, because you do what you will; but are you free to will, or not to will; to desire, or not to desire? Are not your volitions and desires necessarily excited by objects or qualities totally independent of you?

81. "If the actions of men are necessary, if men are not free, by what right does

society punish criminals? Is it not very unjust to chastise beings, who could not act otherwise than they have done?" If the wicked act necessarily according to the impulses of their evil nature, society, in punishing them, acts necessarily by the desire of self-preservation. Certain objects necessarily produce in us the sensation of pain; our nature then forces us against them, and avert them from us. A tiger, pressed by hunger, springs upon the man, whom he wishes to devour; but this man is not master of his fear, and necessarily seeks means to destroy the tiger.

82. "If every thing be necessary, the errors, opinions, and ideas of men are fatal; and, if so, how or why should we attempt to reform them?" The errors of men are necessary consequences of ignorance. Their ignorance, prejudice, and credulity are necessary consequences of their inexperience, negligence, and want of reflection, in the same manner as delirium or lethargy are necessary effects of certain diseases. Truth, experience, reflection, and reason, are remedies calculated to cure ignorance, fanaticism and follies. But, you will ask, why does not truth produce this effect upon many disordered minds? It is because some diseases resist all remedies; because it is impossible to cure obstinate patients, who refuse the remedies presented to them; because the interest of some men, and the folly of others, necessarily oppose the admission of truth.

A cause produces its effect only when its action is not interrupted by stronger causes, which then weakens or render useless, the action of the former. It is impossible that the best arguments should be adopted by men, who are interested in error, prejudiced in its favour, and who decline all reflection; but truth must necessarily undeceive honest minds, who seek her sincerely. Truth is a cause; it necessarily produces its effects, when its impulse is not intercepted by causes, which suspend its effects.

83. "To deprive man of his free will," it is said, "makes him a mere machine, an automaton. Without liberty, he will no longer have either merit or virtue." What is merit in man? It is a manner of acting, which renders him estimable in the eyes of his fellow-beings. What is virtue? It is a disposition, which inclines us to do good to others. What can there be contemptible in machines, or automatons, capable of producing effects so desirable? Marcus Aurelius was useful to the vast Roman Empire. By what right would a machine despise a machine, whose springs facilitate its action? Good men are springs, which second society in its tendency to

happiness; the wicked are ill-formed springs, which disturb the order, progress, and harmony of society. If, for its own utility, society cherishes and rewards the good, it also harasses and destroys the wicked, as useless or hurtful.

84. The world is a necessary agent. All the beings, that compose it, are united to each other, and cannot act otherwise than they do, so long as they are moved by the same causes, and endued with the same properties. When they lose properties, they will necessarily act in a different way. God himself, admitting his existence, cannot be considered a free agent. If there existed a God, his manner of acting would necessarily be determined by the properties inherent in his nature; nothing would be capable of arresting or altering his will. This being granted, neither our actions, prayers, nor sacrifices could suspend, or change his invariable conduct and immutable designs; whence we are forced to infer, that all religion would be useless.

85. Were not divines in perpetual contradiction with themselves, they would see, that, according to their hypothesis, man cannot be reputed free an instant. Do they not suppose man continually dependent on his God? Are we free, when we cannot exist and be preserved without God, and when we cease to exist at the pleasure of his supreme will? If God has made man out of nothing; if his preservation is a continued creation; if God cannot, an instant, lose sight of his creature; if whatever happens to him, is an effect of the divine will; if man can do nothing of himself; if all the events, which he experiences, are effects of the divine decrees; if he does no good without grace from on high, how can they maintain, that a man enjoys a moment's liberty? If God did not preserve him in the moment of sin, how could man sin? If God then preserves him, God forces him to exist, that he may sin.

86. The Divinity is frequently compared to a king, whose revolted subjects are the greater part of mankind; and it is said, he has a right to reward the subjects who remain faithful to him, and to punish the rebellious. This comparison is not just in any of its parts. God presides over a machine, every spring of which he has created. These springs act agreeable to the manner, in which God has formed them; he ought to impute it to his own unskilfulness, if these springs do not contribute to the harmony of the machine, into which it was his will to insert them. God is a created king, who has created to himself subjects of every description; who has formed them according to his own pleasure whose will can never find resistance.

If God has rebellious subjects in his empire, it is because God has resolved to have rebellious subjects. If the sins of men disturb the order of the world, it is because it is the will of God that this order should be disturbed.

Nobody dares to call in question the divine justice; yet, under the government of a just God, we see nothing but acts of injustice and violence. Force decides the fate of nations, equity seems banished from the earth; a few men sport, unpunished, with the peace, property, liberty, and life of others. All is disorder in a world governed by a God who is said to be infinitely displeased with disorder.

87. Although men are for ever admiring the wisdom, goodness, justice, and beautiful order of Providence, they are, in reality, never satisfied with it. Do not the prayers, continually addressed to heaven, shew, that men are by no means satisfied with the divine dispensations? To pray to God for a favour, shews diffidence of his watchful care; to pray to him to avert or put an end to an evil, is to endeavour to obstruct the course of his justice; to implore the assistance of God in our calamities, is to address the author himself of these calamities, to represent to him, that he ought, for our sake, to rectify his plan, which does not accord with our interest.

The Optimist, or he who maintains that *all is well*, and who incessantly cries that we live in *the best world possible*, to be consistent, should never pray; neither ought he to expect another world, where man will be happier. Can there be a better world than *the best world possible*? Some theologians have treated the Optimists as impious, for having intimated that God could not produce a better world, than that in which we live. According to these doctors, it is to limit the power of God, and to offer him insult. But do not these divines see, that it shews much less indignity to God, to assert that he has done his best in producing this world, than to say, that, being able to produce a better, he has had malice enough to produce a very bad one? If the Optimist, by his system, detracts from the divine power, the theologian, who treats him as a blasphemer, is himself a blasphemer, who offends the goodness of God in espousing the cause of his omnipotence.

88. When we complain of the evils, of which our world is the theatre, we are referred to the other world, where it is said, God will make reparation for all the iniquity and misery, which, for a time, he permits here below. But if God, suffering his eternal justice to remain at rest for a long time, could consent to evil during the whole continuance of our present world, what assurance have we, that, during the

continuance of another world, divine justice will not, in like manner, sleep over the misery of its inhabitants?

The divines console us for our sufferings by saying, that God is patient, and that his justice, though often slow, is not the less sure. But do they not see, that patience is incompatible with a just, immutable, and omnipotent being? Can God then permit injustice, even for an instant? To temporize with a known evil, announces either weakness, uncertainty, or collusion. To tolerate evil, when one has power to prevent it, is to consent to the commission of evil.

89. Divines every where exclaim, that God is infinitely just; but that *his justice is not the justice of man*. Of what kind or nature then is this divine justice? What idea can I form of a justice, which so often resembles injustice? Is it not to confound all ideas of just and unjust, to say, that what is equitable in God is iniquitous in his creatures? How can we receive for our model a being, whose divine perfections are precisely the reverse of human?

"God," it is said, "is sovereign arbiter of our destinies. His supreme power, which nothing can limit, justly permits him to do with the works of his own hands according to his good pleasure. A worm, like man, has no right even to complain." This arrogant style is evidently borrowed from the language, used by the ministers of tyrants, when they stop the mouths of those who suffer from their violences. It cannot then be the language of the ministers of a God, whose equity is highly extolled; it is not made to be imposed upon a being, who reasons. Ministers of a just God! I will inform you then, that the greatest power cannot confer upon your God himself the right of being unjust even to the vilest of his creatures. A despot is not a God. A God, who arrogates to himself the right of doing evil, is a tyrant; a tyrant is not a model for men; he must be an object execrable to their eyes.

Is it not indeed strange, that in order to justify the Divinity, they make him every moment the most unjust of beings! As soon as we complain of his conduct, they think to silence us by alleging, that *God is master*; which signifies, that God, being the strongest, is not bound by ordinary rules. But the right of the strongest is the violation of all rights. It seems right only to the eyes of a savage conqueror, who in the heat of his fury imagines, that he may do whatever he pleases with the unfortunate victims, whom he has conquered. This barbarous right can appear legitimate only to slaves blind enough to believe that everything is lawful to tyrants whom they feel too weak to resist.

In the greatest calamities, do not devout persons, through a ridiculous simplicity, or rather a sensible contradiction in terms, exclaim, that *the Almighty is master*. Thus, inconsistent reasoners, believe, that the *Almighty* (a Being, one of whose first attributes is goodness,) sends you pestilence, war, and famine! You believe that the *Almighty*, this good being, has the will and right to inflict the greatest evils, you can bear! Cease, at least, to call your God *good*, when he does you evil; say not, that he is just, say that he is the strongest, and that it is impossible for you to ward off the blows of his caprice.

God, say you, *chastises only for our good*. But what real good can result to a people from being exterminated by the plague, ravaged by wars, corrupted by the examples of perverse rulers, continually crushed under the iron sceptre of a succession of merciless tyrants, annihilated by the scourges of a bad government, whose destructive effects are often felt for ages? If chastisements are good, then they cannot have too much of a good thing! *The eyes of faith* must be strange eyes, if with them they see advantages in the most dreadful calamities, in the vices and follies with which our species are afflicted.

90. What strange ideas of divine justice must Christians have, who are taught to believe, that their God, in view of reconciling to himself the human race, guilty, though unconscious, of the sin of their fathers, has put to death his own son, who was innocent and incapable of sinning? What should we say of a king, whose subjects should revolt, and who, to appease himself, should find no other expedient than to put to death the heir of his crown, who had not participated in the general rebellion? "It is," the Christian will say, "through goodness to his subjects, unable of themselves to satisfy divine justice, that God has consented to the cruel death of his son." But the goodness of a father to strangers does not give him the right of being unjust and barbarous to his own son. All the qualities, which theology ascribes to God, reciprocally destroy one another. The exercise of one of his perfections is always at the expense of the exercise of another.

Has the Jew more rational ideas of divine justice than the Christian? The pride of a king kindles the anger of heaven; *Jehovah* causes the pestilence to descend upon his innocent people; seventy thousand subjects are exterminated to expiate the fault of a monarch, whom the goodness of God resolved to spare.

91. Notwithstanding the various acts of injustice, with which all religions delight to blacken the Divinity, men cannot consent to accuse him of iniquity. They fear, that, like the tyrants of this world, truth will offend him, and redouble upon them the weight of his malice and tyranny. They hearken therefore to their priests, who tell them, that their God is a tender father; that this God is an equitable monarch whose object in this world is to assure himself of the love, obedience and respect of his subjects; who gives them liberty of acting only to afford them an opportunity of meriting his favours, and of acquiring an eternal happiness, which he does not owe them. By what signs can men discover the tenderness of a father, who has given life to the greater part of his children merely to drag out upon the earth a painful, restless, bitter existence? Is there a more unfortunate present, than that pretended liberty, which, we are told, men are very liable to abuse, and thereby to incur eternal misery?

92. By calling mortals to life, what a cruel and dangerous part has not the Deity forced them to act? Thrown into the world without their consent, provided with a temperament of which they are not masters, animated by passions and desires inherent in their nature, exposed to snares which they have not power to escape, hurried away by events which they could not foresee or prevent, unhappy mortals are compelled to run a career, which may lead them to punishments horrible in duration and violence.

Travellers inform us, that, in Asia, a Sultan reigned, full of fantastical ideas, and very absolute in his whims. By a strange madness, this prince spent his time seated at a table, upon which were placed three dice and a dice-box. One end of the table was covered with pieces of silver, designed to excite the avarice of his courtiers and people. He, knowing the foible of his subjects, addresses them as follows: Slaves, I wish your happiness. My goodness proposes to enrich you, and make you all happy. Do you see these treasures? Well, they are for you; strive to gain them; let each, in his turn, take the box and dice; whoever has the fortune to throw sixes, shall be master of the treasure. But, I forewarn you, that he who has not the happiness to throw the number required, shall be precipitated for ever into a dark dungeon, where my justice demands that he be burned with a slow fire. Upon this discourse of the monarch, the company look at each other affrighted. No one wishes to expose himself to so dangerous a chance. What! says the enraged Sultan, does no one offer to play? I tell you then you must; My glory requires that you should play. Play then; obey without replying. It is well to observe, that the dice of the despot are so prepared, that out of a hundred thousand throws, there is but one, which can gain the number required. Thus the generous monarch has the pleasure of seeing his prison well filled, and his riches seldom ravished from him. Mortals! this SULTAN is your GOD; his TREASURE IS HEAVEN; his DUNGEON IS HELL, and it is you who hold the DICE!

93. Divines repeatedly assure us, that we owe Providence infinite gratitude for the numberless blessings it bestows. They loudly extol the happiness of existence. But, alas! how many mortals are truly satisfied with their mode of existence? If life has sweets, with how much bitterness is it not mixed? Does not a single chagrin often suffice suddenly to poison the most peaceable and fortunate life? Are there many, who, if it were in their power would begin again, at the same price, the painful career, in which, without their consent, destiny has placed them?

They say, that existence is a great blessing. But is not this existence continually troubled with fears, and maladies, often cruel and little deserved? May not this existence, threatened on so many sides, be torn from us any moment? Where is the man, who has not been deprived of a dear wife, beloved child, or consoling friend, whose loss every moment intrudes upon his thoughts? There are few, who have not been forced to drink of the cup of misfortune; there are few, who have not desired their end. Finally, it did not depend upon us to exist or not to exist. Should the bird then be very grateful to the fowler for taking him in his net and confining him in his cage for his diversion?

94. Notwithstanding the infirmities and misery which man is forced to undergo, he has, nevertheless, the folly to think himself the favourite of his God, the object of all his cares, the sole end of all his works. He imagines, that the whole universe is made for him; he arrogantly calls himself the *king of nature*, and values himself far above other animals. Mortal! upon what canst thou found thy haughty pretensions? It is, sayest thou, upon thy soul, upon thy reason, upon the sublime faculties, which enable thee to exercise an absolute empire over the beings, which surround thee. But, weak sovereign of the world; art thou sure, one moment, of the continuance of thy reign? Do not the smallest atoms of matter, which thou despisest, suffice to tear thee from thy throne, and deprive thee of life? Finally, does not

the king of animals at last become the food of worms? Thou speakest of thy soul! But dost thou know what a soul is? Dost thou not see, that this soul is only the assemblage of thy organs, from which results life? Wouldst thou then refuse a soul to other animals, who live, think, judge, and compare, like thee; who seek pleasure, and avoid pain, like thee; and who often have organs, which serve them better than thine? Thou boastest of thy intellectual faculties; but do these faculties, of which thou art so proud, make thee happier than other animals? Dost thou often make use of that reason, in which thou gloriest, and to which religion commands thee not to listen? Are those brutes, which thou disdainest, because they are less strong or less cunning than thou art, subject to mental pains, to a thousand frivolous passions, to a thousand imaginary wants, to which thou art a continual prey? Are they, like thee, tormented by the past, alarmed at the future? Confined solely to the present, does not what you call their *instinct*, and what I call their *intelligence*, suffice to preserve and defend them, and to supply them with all they want? Does not this instinct, of which thou speakest with contempt, often serve them better than thy wonderful faculties? Is not their peaceful ignorance more advantageous to them, than those extravagant meditations and worthless researches, which render thee unhappy, and for which thy zeal urges thee even to massacre the beings of thy noble species? Finally, have these beasts, like so many mortals, a troubled imagination, which makes them fear, not only death, but likewise eternal torments?

Augustus, hearing that Herod, king of Judea, had put his sons to death, exclaimed: *It is much better to be Herod's hog, than his son*. As much may be said of man. This dear child of Providence runs far greater risks than all other animals; having suffered much in this world, does he not imagine, that he is in danger of suffering eternally in another?

95. Where is the precise line of distinction between man and the animals whom he calls brutes? In what does he differ essentially from beasts? It is, we are told, by his intelligence, by the faculties of his mind, and by his reason, that man appears superior to all other animals, who, in all their actions, move only by physical impulses, in which reason has no share. But finally, brutes, having fewer wants than man, easily do without his intellectual faculties, which would be perfectly useless in their mode of existence. Their instinct is sufficient; while all the faculties of man scarcely suffice to render his existence supportable, and to satisfy the wants,

which his imagination and his prejudices multiply to his torment.

Brutes are not influenced by the same objects, as man; they have not the same wants, desires, nor fancies; and they very soon arrive to maturity, while the mind of man seldom attains to the full enjoyment and free exercise of its faculties and to such a use of them, as is conducive to his happiness.

96. We are assured, that the human soul is a simple substance. It should then be the same in every individual, each having the same intellectual faculties; yet this is not the case. Men differ as much in the qualities of the mind, as in the features of the face. There are human beings as different from one another, as man is from a horse or a dog. What conformity or resemblance do we find between some men? What an infinite distance is there between the genius of a Locke or a Newton, and that of a peasant, Hottentot, or Laplander?

Man differs from other animals only in his organization, which enables him to produce effects, of which animals are not capable. The variety, observable in the organs of individuals of the human species suffices to explain the differences in what is called their intellectual faculties. More or less delicacy in these organs, warmth in the blood, mobility in the fluids, flexibility or stiffness in the fibres and nerves, must necessarily produce the infinite diversity, which we observe in the minds of men. It is by exercise, habit and education, that the mind is unfolded and becomes superior to that of others. Man, without culture and experience, is as void of reason and industry, as the brute. A stupid man is one, whose organs move with difficulty, whose brain does not easily vibrate, whose blood circulates slowly. A man of genius is he, whose organs are flexible, whose sensations are quick, whose brain vibrates with celerity. A learned man is he, whose organs and brain have been long exercised upon objects to which he is devoted.

Without culture, experience, or reason, is not man more contemptible and worthy of hatred, than the vilest insects or most ferocious beasts? Is there in nature a more detestable being, than a Tiberius, a Nero, or a Caligula? Have those destroyers of the human race, known by the name of conquerors, more estimable souls than bears, lions, or panthers? Are there animals in the world more detestable than tyrants?

97. The superiority which man so gratuitously arrogates to himself over other animals, soon vanishes in the light of reason, when we reflect on human extrava-

gances. How many animals shew more mildness, reflection, and reason, than the animal, who calls himself reasonable above all others? Are there among men, so often enslaved and oppressed, societies as well constituted as those of the ants, bees, or beavers? Do we ever see ferocious beasts of the same species mangle and destroy one another without profit? Do we ever see religious wars among them? The cruelty of beasts towards other species arises from hunger, the necessity of nourishment; the cruelty of man towards man arises only from the vanity of his masters and the folly of his impertinent prejudices. Speculative men, who endeavour to make us believe, that all in the universe was made for man, are much embarrassed, when we ask, how so many hurtful animals can contribute to the happiness of man? What known advantage results to the friend of the gods, from being bitten by a viper, stung by a gnat, devoured by vermin, torn in pieces by a tiger, etc.? Would not all these animals reason as justly as our theologians, should they pretend that man was made for them?

98. AN EASTERN TALE.

At some distance from Bagdad, a hermit, renowned for his sanctity, passed his days in an agreeable solitude. The neighbouring inhabitants, to obtain an interest in his prayers, daily flocked to his hermitage, to carry him provisions and presents. The holy man, without ceasing, gave thanks to God for the blessings, with which providence loaded him. "O Allah!" said he, "how ineffable is thy love to thy servants. What have I done to merit the favours, that I receive from thy bounty? O Monarch of the skies! O Father of nature! what praises could worthily celebrate thy munificence, and thy paternal care! O Allah! how great is thy goodness to the children of men!" Penetrated with gratitude, the hermit made a vow to undertake, for the seventh time, a pilgrimage to Mecca. The war which then raged between the Persians and Turks, could not induce him to defer his pious enterprise. Full of confidence in God, he sets out under the inviolable safeguard of a religious habit. He passes through the hostile troops without any obstacle; far from being molested, he receives, at every step, marks of veneration from the soldiers of the two parties. At length, borne down with fatigue, he is obliged to seek refuge against the rays of a scorching sun; he rests under the cool shade of a group of palm-trees. In this solitary place, the man of God finds not only an enchanting retreat, but a delicious repast. He has only to put forth his hand to gather dates and other pleasant fruits;

a brook affords him the means of quenching his thirst. A green turf invites him to sleep; upon waking he performs the sacred ablution, and exclaims in a transport of joy: "O Allah! how great is thy goodness to the children of men!" After this perfect refreshment, the saint, full of strength and gaiety, pursues his way; it leads him across a smiling country, which presents to his eyes flowery hillocks, enamelled meadows, and trees loaded with fruit. Affected by this sight, he ceases not to adore the rich and liberal hand of providence, which appears every where providing for the happiness of the human race. Going a little farther, the mountains are pretty difficult to pass; but having once arrived at the summit, a hideous spectacle suddenly appears to his view. His soul is filled with horror. He discovers a vast plain laid waste with fire and sword; he beholds it covered with hundreds of carcases, the deplorable remains of a bloody battle, lately fought upon this field. Eagles, vultures, ravens and wolves were greedily devouring the dead bodies with which the ground was covered. This sight plunges our pilgrim into a gloomy meditation. Heaven, by special favour, had enabled him to understand the language of beasts. He heard a wolf, gorged with human flesh, cry out in the excess of his joy: "O Allah! how great is thy goodness to the children of wolves. Thy provident wisdom takes care to craze the minds of these detestable men, who are so dangerous to our species. By an effect of thy Providence, which watches over thy creatures, these destroyers cut one another's throats, and furnish us with sumptuous meals. O Allah! how great is thy goodness to the children of wolves!"

99. A heated imagination sees in the universe only the blessings of heaven; a calmer mind finds in it both good and evil. "I exist," say you; but is this existence always a good? "Behold," you say, "that sun, which lights; this earth, which for you is covered with crops and verdure; these flowers, which bloom to regale your senses; these trees, which bend under the weight of delicious fruits; these pure waters, which run only to quench your thirst; those seas, which embrace the universe to facilitate your commerce; these animals, which a foreseeing nature provides for your use." Yes; I see all these things, and I enjoy them. But in many climates, this beautiful sun is almost always hidden; in others, its excessive heat torments, creates storms, produces frightful diseases, and parches the fields; the pastures are without verdure, the trees without fruit, the crops are scorched, the springs are dried up; I can only with difficulty subsist, and now complain of the cruelties of nature, which

to you always appears so beneficent. If these seas bring me spices, and useless commodities, do they not destroy numberless mortals, who are foolish enough to seek them? The vanity of man persuades him, that he is the sole center of the universe; he creates for himself a world and a God; he thinks himself of sufficient consequence to derange nature at his pleasure. But, concerning other animals, he reasons like an atheist. Does he not imagine, that the individuals different from his own are automatons unworthy of the blessings of universal providence, and that brutes cannot be objects of his justice or goodness? Mortals regard the happy or unhappy events, health or sickness, life or death, plenty or want, as rewards or punishments for the right use or abuse of the liberty, with which they erroneously imagine themselves endowed. Do they reason in the same manner concerning the brutes? No. Although they see them, under a just God, enjoy and suffer, equally subject to health and sickness, live and die, like themselves, it never occurs to them to ask by what crime, these beasts could have incurred the displeasure of their Creator? Have not men, blinded by their religious prejudices, in order to free themselves from embarrassment, carried their folly so far as to pretend that beasts have no feeling?

Will men never renounce their foolish pretensions? Will they never acknowledge that nature is not made for them? Will they never see that nature has placed equality among all beings she has produced? Will they never perceive that all organized beings are equally made to be born and die, enjoy and suffer? Finally, far from having any cause to be puffed up with their mental faculties, are they not forced to grant, that these faculties often make them more unhappy than beasts, in which we find neither opinions, prejudices, vanities, nor follies, which every moment decide the welfare of man?

100. The superiority which men arrogate over other animals, is chiefly founded upon their opinion, that they have the exclusive possession of an immortal soul. But ask them what this soul is, and they are puzzled. They will say, it is an unknown substance-- a secret power distinct from their bodies--a spirit, of which they have no idea. Ask them how this spirit, which they suppose to be like their God wholly void of extension, could combine itself with their material bodies, and they will tell you, they know nothing about it; that it is to them a mystery; that this combination is an effect of the omnipotence of God. These are the ideas that men form of the hidden, or rather imaginary substance, which they consider as the main

spring of all their actions!

If the soul is a substance essentially different from the body, and can have no relation to it, their union would be, not a mystery, but an impossibility. Besides, this soul being of a nature different from the body, must necessarily act in a different manner; yet we see that this pretended soul is sensible of the motions experienced by the body, and that these two substances, essentially different, always acts in concert. You will say that this harmony is also a mystery. But I will tell you, that I see not my soul, that I know and am sensible of my body only, that it is this body which feels, thinks, judges, suffers, and enjoys; and that all these faculties are necessary results of its own mechanism, or organization.

101. Although it is impossible for men to form the least idea of the soul, or the pretended spirit, which animates them; yet they persuade themselves that this unknown soul is exempt from death. Every thing proves to them, that they feel, that they think, that they acquire ideas, that they enjoy and suffer, only by means of the senses, or material organs of the body. Admitting even the existence of this soul, they cannot help acknowledging, that it depends entirely upon the body, and undergoes, all its vicissitudes; and yet it is imagined, that this soul has nothing, in its nature, similar to the body; that it can act and feel without the assistance of the body; in a word, that this soul, freed from the body, and disengaged from its senses, can live, enjoy, suffer, experience happiness, or feel excruciating torments. Upon such a tissue of absurdities is built the marvellous opinion of the *immortality of the soul*. If I ask, what are the motives for believing the soul immortal, they immediately answer, that it is because man naturally desires to be immortal: but, because you desire a thing ardently, can you infer that your desire will be fulfilled? By what strange logic can we dare affirm, that a thing cannot fail to happen, because we ardently desire it? Are desires, begotten by the imagination, the measure of reality? The impious, you say, deprived of the flattering hope of another life, wish to be annihilated. Very well: may they not then as justly conclude, from *their* desire, that they shall be annihilated, as you may conclude from *your* desire, that you shall exist for ever.

102. Man dies, and the human body after death is no longer anything but a mass incapable of producing those motions, of which the sum total constituted life. We see, that it has no longer circulation, respiration, digestion, speech, or thought.

It is pretended, that the soul is then separated from the body; but to say, that this soul, with which we are unacquainted, is the principle of life, is to say nothing, unless that an unknown power is the hidden principle of imperceptible movements. Nothing is more natural and simple, than to believe, that the dead man no longer lives: nothing is more extravagant, than to believe, that the dead man is still alive. We laugh at the simplicity of some nations, whose custom is to bury provision with the dead, under an idea that it will be useful and necessary to them in the other life. Is it then more ridiculous or absurd to suppose, that men will eat after death, than to imagine, that they will think, that they will be actuated by agreeable or disagreeable ideas, that they will enjoy or suffer, and that they will experience repentance or delight, after the organs, adapted to produce sensations or ideas, are once dissolved. To say that the souls of men will be happy or unhappy after death, is in other words to say, that men will see without eyes, hear without ears, taste without palates, smell without noses, and touch without hands. And persons, who consider themselves very reasonable, adopt these ideas!

103. The dogma of the immortality of the soul supposes the soul to be a simple substance; in a word, a spirit. But I ask again, what is a spirit? "It is," say you, "a substance void of extension, incorruptible, having nothing common with matter." If so, how is your soul born, and how does it grow, how does it strengthen or weaken itself, how does it get disordered and grow old, in the same progression as your body?

To all these questions you answer, that these are mysteries. If so, you cannot understand them. If you cannot understand them, why do you decide about a thing, of which you are unable to form the least idea? To believe or affirm any thing, it is necessary, at least, to know in what it consists. To believe in the existence of your immaterial soul, is to say, that you are persuaded of the existence of a thing, of which it is impossible for you to form any true notion; it is to believe in words without meaning. To affirm that the thing is as you say, is the height of folly or vanity.

104. Are not theologians strange reasoners? Whenever they cannot divine the *natural* causes of things, they invent what they call *supernatural*; such as spirits, occult causes, inexplicable agents, or rather *words*, much more obscure than the *things* they endeavour to explain. Let us remain in nature, when we wish to

account for the phenomena of nature; let us be content to remain ignorant of causes too delicate for our organs; and let us be persuaded, that, by going beyond nature, we shall never solve the problems which nature presents.

Even upon the hypothesis of theology, (that is, supposing an all-powerful mover of matter,) by what right would theologians deny, that their God has power to give this matter the faculty of thought? Was it then more difficult for him to create combinations of matter, from which thought might result, than spirits who could think? At least, by supposing matter, which thinks, we should have some notions of the subject of thought, or of what thinks in us; whereas, by attributing thought to an immaterial being, it is impossible to form the least idea of it.

105. It is objected against us, that materialism makes man a mere machine, which is said to be very dishonourable. But, will it be much more honourable for man, if we should say, that he acts by the secret impulses of a spirit, or by a certain *I know not what*, that animates him in a manner totally inexplicable.

It is easy to perceive, that the supposed superiority of *spirit* over matter, or of the soul over the body, has no other foundation than men's ignorance of this soul, while they are more familiarized with *matter*, with which they imagine they are acquainted, and of which they think they can discern the origin. But the most simple movements of our bodies are to every man, who studies them, as inexplicable as thought.

106. The high value, which so many people set upon spiritual substance, has no other motive than their absolute inability to define it intelligibly. The contempt shewn for *matter* by our metaphysicians, arises only from the circumstance, that familiarity begets contempt. When they tell us, that *the soul is more excellent and noble than the body*, they say what they know not.

107. The dogma of another life is incessantly extolled, as useful. It is maintained, that even though it should be only a fiction, it is advantageous, because it deceives men, and conducts them to virtue. But is it true, that this dogma makes men wiser and more virtuous? Are the nations, who believe this fiction, remarkable for purity of morals? Has not the visible world ever the advantage over the invisible? If those, who are trusted with the instruction and government of men, had knowledge and virtue themselves, they would govern them much better by realities, than by fictions. But crafty, ambitious and corrupt legislators, have every

where found it better to amuse with fables, than to teach them truths, to unfold their reason, to excite them to virtue by sensible and real motives, in fine, to govern them in a rational manner. Priests undoubtedly had reasons for making the soul immaterial; they wanted souls to people the imaginary regions, which they have discovered in the other life. Material souls would, like all bodies, have been subject to dissolution. Now, if men should believe, that all must perish with the body, the geographers of the other world would evidently lose the right of guiding men's souls towards that unknown abode; they would reap no profits from the hope with which they feed them, and the terrors with which they oppress them. If futurity is of no real utility to mankind, it is, at least, of the greatest utility to those, who have assumed the office of conducting them thither.

108. "But," it will be said, "is not the dogma of the immortality of the soul comforting to beings, who are often very unhappy here below? Though it should be an error, is it not pleasing? Is it not a blessing to man to believe, that he shall be able to enjoy hereafter a happiness, which is denied him upon earth?" Thus, poor mortals! you make your wishes the measure of truth; because you desire to live for ever, and to be happier, you at once conclude, that you shall live for ever, and that you shall be more fortunate in an unknown world, than in this known world, where you often find nothing but affliction! Consent therefore to leave, without regret, this world which gives the greater part of you much more torment than pleasure. Submit to the order of nature, which demands that you, as well as all other beings, should not endure for ever.

We are incessantly told, that religion has infinite consolations for the unfortunate, that the idea of the soul's immortality, and of a happier life, is very proper to elevate man, and to support him under adversity, which awaits him upon earth. It is said, on the contrary, that materialism is an afflicting system, calculated to degrade man; then it puts him upon a level with the brutes, breaks his courage, and shows him no other prospect than frightful annihilation, capable of driving him to despair and suicide, whenever he is unhappy. The great art of theologians is to blow hot and cold, to afflict and console, to frighten and encourage.

It appears by theological fictions, that the regions of the other life are happy and unhappy. Nothing is more difficult than to become worthy of the abode of felicity; nothing more easy than to obtain a place in the abode of torment, which

God is preparing for the unfortunate victims of eternal fury. Have those then, who think the other life so pleasant and flattering, forgotten, that according to them, that life is to be attended with torments to the greater part of mortals? Is not the idea of total annihilation infinitely preferable to the idea of an eternal existence, attended with anguish and *gnashing of teeth*? Is the fear of an end more afflicting, than that of having had a beginning! The fear of ceasing to exist is a real evil only to the imagination, which alone begat the dogma of another life.

Christian ministers say that the idea of a happier life is joyous. Admitted. Every person would desire a more agreeable existence than that he enjoys here. But, if paradise is inviting, you will grant, that hell is frightful. Heaven is very difficult, and hell very easy to be merited. Do you not say, that a *narrow* way leads to the happy regions, and a *broad* way to the regions of misery? Do you not often say, that *the number of the elect is very small, and that of the reprobate very large*? Is not Grace, which your God grants but to a very few, necessary to salvation? Now, I assure you, that these ideas are by no means consoling; that I had rather be annihilated, once for all, than to burn for ever; that the fate of beasts is to me more desirable than that of the damned; that the opinion which relieves me from afflicting fears in this world, appears to me more joyous, than the uncertainty arising from the opinion of a God, who, master of his grace, grants it to none but his favourites, and permits all others to become worthy of eternal torment. Nothing but enthusiasm or folly can induce a man to prefer improbable conjectures, attended with uncertainty and insupportable fears.

109. All religious principles are the work of pure imagination, in which experience and reason have no share. It is extremely difficult to combat them, because the imagination, once prepossessed by chimeras, which astonish or disturb it, is incapable of reasoning. To combat religion and its phantoms with the arms of reason, is like using a sword to kill gnats; as soon as the blow is struck, the gnats and chimeras come hovering round again, and resume in the mind the place, from which they were thought to have been for ever banished.

When we reject, as too weak, the proofs given of the existence of a God, they instantly oppose to the arguments, which destroy that existence, an *inward sense*, a deep persuasion, an invincible inclination, born in every man, which holds up to his mind, in spite of himself, the idea of an almighty being, whom he cannot entirely expel from his mind, and whom he is compelled to acknowledge, in spite of the strongest reasons that can be urged. But whoever will analyse this *inward sense*, upon which such stress is laid, will perceive, that it is only the effect of a rooted habit, which, shutting their eyes against the most demonstrative proofs, subjects the greater part of men, and often even the most enlightened, to the prejudices of childhood. What avails this inward sense, or this deep persuasion, against the evidence, which demonstrates, that *whatever implies a contradiction cannot exist*?

We are gravely assured, that the non-existence of God is not demonstrated. Yet, by all that men have hitherto said of him, nothing is better demonstrated, than that this God is a chimera, whose existence is totally impossible; since nothing is more evident, than that a being cannot possess qualities so unlike, so contradictory, so irreconcilable, as those, which every religion upon earth attributes to the Divinity. Is not the theologian's God, as well as that of the deist, a cause incompatible with the effects attributed to it? Let them do what they will, it is necessary either to invent another God, or to grant, that he, who, for so many ages, has been held up to the terror of mortals, is at the same time very good and very bad, very powerful and very weak, unchangeable and fickle, perfectly intelligent and perfectly void of reason, of order and permitting disorder, very just and most unjust, very skilful and unskilful. In short, are we not forced to confess, that it is impossible to reconcile the discordant attributes, heaped upon a being, of whom we cannot speak without the most palpable contradictions? Let any one attribute a single quality to the Divinity, and it is universally contradicted by the effects, ascribed to this cause.

110. Theology might justly be defined the *science of contradictions*. Every religion is only a system, invented to reconcile irreconcilable notions. By the aid of habit and terror, man becomes obstinate in the greatest absurdities, even after they are exposed in the clearest manner. All religions are easily combated, but with difficulty extirpated. Reason avails nothing against custom, which becomes, says the proverb, *a second nature*. Many persons, in other respects sensible, even after having examined the rotten foundation of their belief, adhere to it in contempt of the most striking arguments. Whenever we complain of religion, its shocking absurdities, and impossibilities, we are told that we are not made to understand the truths of religion; that reason goes astray, and is capable of leading us to perdition; and moreover, that *what is folly in the eyes of man, is wisdom in the eyes of God*, to whom nothing

is impossible. In short, to surmount, by a single word, the most insurmountable difficulties, presented on all sides by theology, they get rid of them by saying, these are *mysteries*!

111. What is a mystery? By examining the thing closely, I soon perceive, that a mystery is nothing but a contradiction, a palpable absurdity, a manifest impossibility, over which theologians would oblige men humbly to shut their eyes. In a word, a mystery is whatever our spiritual guides cannot explain.

It is profitable to the ministers of religion, that people understand nothing of what they teach. It is impossible to examine what we do not comprehend; when we do not see, we must suffer ourselves to be led. If religion were clear, priests would find less business.

Without mysteries there can be no religion; mystery is essential to it; a religion void of mysteries, would be a contradiction in terms. The God, who serves as the foundation of *natural religion*, or *deism*, is himself the greatest of mysteries.

112. Every revealed religion is filled with mysterious dogmas, unintelligible principles, incredible wonders, astonishing recitals, which appear to have been invented solely to confound reason. Every religion announces a hidden God, whose essence is a mystery; consequently, the conduct, ascribed to him, is no less inconceivable than his essence. The Deity has never spoken only in an enigmatical and mysterious manner, in the various religions, which have been founded in different regions of our globe; he has everywhere revealed himself only to announce mysteries; that is, to inform mortals, that he intended they should believe contradictions, impossibilities, and things to which they were incapable of affixing any clear ideas.

The more mysterious and incredible a religion is, the more power it has to please the imagination of men. The darker a religion is, the more it appears divine, that is, conformable to the nature of a hidden being, of whom they have no ideas. Ignorance prefers the unknown, the hidden, the fabulous, the marvellous, the incredible, or even the terrible, to what is clear, simple, and true. Truth does not operate upon the imagination in so lively a manner as fiction, which, in other respects, everyone is able to arrange in his own way. The vulgar like to listen to fables. Priests and legislators, by inventing religions and forging mysteries have served the vulgar people well. They have thereby gained enthusiasts, women and fools. Beings of this stamp are easily satisfied with things, which they are incapable of examining. The love of simplicity and truth is to be found only among the few, whose imagination is regulated by study and reflection.

The inhabitants of a village are never better pleased with their parson, than when he introduces Latin into his sermon. The ignorant always imagine, that he, who speaks to them of things they do not understand, is a learned man. Such is the true principle of the credulity of the people, and of the authority of those, who pretend to guide nations.

113. To announce mysteries to men, is to give and withhold; it is to talk in order not to be understood. He, who speaks only obscurely, either seeks to amuse himself by the embarrassment, which he causes, or finds his interest in not explaining himself too clearly. All secrecy indicates distrust, impotence, and fear. Princes and their ministers make a mystery of their projects, for fear their enemies should discover and render them abortive. Can a good God amuse himself by perplexing his creatures? What interest then could he have in commanding his ministers to announce riddles and mysteries?

It is said, that man, by the weakness of his nature, is totally incapable of understanding the divine dispensations, which can be to him only a series of mysteries; God cannot disclose to him secrets, necessarily above his reach. If so, I answer again, that man is not made to attend to the divine dispensations; that these dispensations are to him by no means interesting; that he has no need of mysteries, which he cannot understand; and consequently, that a mysterious religion is no more fit for him, than an eloquent discourse is for a flock of sheep.

114. The Deity has revealed himself with so little uniformity in the different countries of our globe, that in point of religion, men regard one another with hatred and contempt. The partisans of the different sects think each other very ridiculous and foolish. Mysteries, most revered in one religion, are objects of derision to another. God, in revealing himself to mankind, ought at least, to have spoken the same language to all, and saved their feeble minds the perplexity of inquiring which religion really emanated from him, or what form of worship is most acceptable in his sight.

A universal God ought to have revealed a universal religion. By what fatality then are there so many different religions upon earth? Which is really right, among the great number of those, each of which exclusively pretends to be the true one? There is great reason to believe, that no religion enjoys this advantage. Division and disputes upon opinions are indubitable signs of the uncertainty and obscurity of the principles, upon which they build.

115. If religion were necessary at all, it ought to be intelligible to all. If this religion were the most important concern of men, the goodness of God would seem to demand, that it should be to them of all things the most clear, evident, and demonstrative. Is it not then astonishing, that this thing so essential to the happiness of mortals, is precisely that, which they understand least, and about which, for so many ages, their teachers have most disputed? Priests have never agreed upon the manner of understanding the will of a God, who has revealed himself.

The world, may be compared to a public fair, in which are several empirics, each of whom endeavours to attract the passengers by decrying the remedies sold by his brothers. Each shop has its customers, who are persuaded, that their quacks possess the only true remedies; and notwithstanding a continual use of them, they perceive not the inefficacy of these remedies, or that they are as infirm as those, who run after the quacks of a different shop.

Devotion is a disorder of the imagination contracted in infancy. The devout man is a hypochondriac, who only augments his malady by the application of remedies. The wise man abstains from them entirely; he pays attention to his diet, and in other respects leaves nature to her course.

116. To a man of sense, nothing appears more ridiculous, than the opinions, which the partisans of the different religions with equal folly entertain of each other. A Christian regards the *Koran*, that is, the divine revelation announced by Mahomet, as nothing but a tissue of impertinent reveries, and impostures insulting to the divinity. The Mahometan, on the other hand, treats the Christian as an *idolater* and a *dog*. He sees nothing but absurdities in his religion. He imagines he has a right to subdue the Christian, and to force him, sword in hand, to receive the religion of his divine prophet. Finally, he believes, that nothing is more impious and unreasonable, than to worship a man, or to believe in the Trinity. The *protestant* Christian who without scruple worships a man, and firmly believes the inconceivable mystery of the *trinity*, ridicules the *catholic* Christian for believing in the mystery of *transubstantiation*; he considers him mad, impious, and idolatrous, because

he kneels to worship some bread, in which he thinks he sees God. Christians of every sect regard, as silly stories, the incarnations of *Vishnu*, the God of the Indies; they maintain, that the only true *incarnation* is that of *Jesus*, son of a carpenter. The deist, who calls himself the follower of a religion, which he supposes to be that of nature, content with admitting a God, of whom he has no idea, makes a jest of all the mysteries, taught by the various religions in the world.

117. Is there any thing more contradictory, impossible, or mysterious, than the creation of matter by an immaterial being, who, though immutable, operates continual changes in the world? Is any thing more incompatible with every notion of common sense, than to believe, that a supremely good, wise, equitable and powerful being presides over nature, and by himself directs the movements of a world, full of folly, misery, crimes and disorders, which by a single word, he could have prevented or removed? In fine, whenever we admit a being as contradictory as the God of theology, how can we reject the most improbable fables, astonishing miracles, and profound mysteries.

118. The Deist exclaims: "Abstain from worshipping the cruel and capricious God of theology; mine is a being infinitely wise and good; he is the father of men, the mildest of sovereigns; it is he who fills the universe with his benefits." But do you not see that every thing in this world contradicts the good qualities, which you ascribe to your God? In the numerous family of this tender father, almost all are unhappy. Under the government of this just sovereign, vice is triumphant, and virtue in distress. Among those blessings you extol, and which only enthusiasm can see, I behold a multitude of evils, against which you obstinately shut your eyes. Forced to acknowledge, that your beneficent God, in contradiction with himself, distributes good and evil with the same hand, for his justification you must, like the priest, refer me to the regions of another life. Invent, therefore, another God; for yours is no less contradictory than that of theologians.

A good God, who does evil, or consents to the commission of evil; a God full of equity, and in whose empire innocence is often oppressed; a perfect God, who produces none but imperfect and miserable works; are not such a God and his conduct as great mysteries, as that of the incarnation?

You blush for your fellow-citizens, who allow themselves to be persuaded, that the God of the universe could change himself into a man, and die upon a cross in a corner of Asia. The mystery of the incarnation appears to you very absurd. You think nothing more ridiculous, than a God, who transforms himself into bread, and causes himself daily to be eaten in a thousand different places. But are all these mysteries more contradictory to reason than a God, the avenger and rewarder of the actions of men? Is man, according to you, free, or not free? In either case, your God, if he has the shadow of equity, can neither punish nor reward him. If man is free, it is God, who has made him free; therefore God is the primitive cause of all his actions; in punishing him for his faults, he would punish him for having executed what he had given him liberty to do. If man is not free to act otherwise than he does, would not God be most unjust, in punishing man for faults, which he could not help committing.

The minor, or secondary, absurdities, with which all religions abound, are to many people truly striking; but they have not the courage to trace the source of these absurdities. They see not, that a God full of contradictions, caprices and inconsistent qualities, has only served to disorder men's imaginations, and to produce an endless succession of chimeras.

119. The theologian would shut the mouths of those who deny the existence of God, by saying, that all men, in all ages and countries, have acknowledged some divinity or other; that every people have believed in an invisible and powerful being, who has been the object of their worship and veneration; in short, that there is no nation, however savage, who are not persuaded of the existence of some intelligence superior to human nature. But, can an error be changed into truth by the belief of all men? The great philosopher Bayle has justly observed, that "general tradition, or the unanimous consent of mankind, is no criterion of truth."

There was a time, when all men believed that the sun moved round the earth, but this error was detected. There was a time, when nobody believed the existence of the antipodes, and when every one was persecuted, who had temerity enough to maintain it. At present, every informed man firmly believes it. All nations, with the exception of a few men who are less credulous than the rest, still believe in ghosts and spirits. No sensible man now adopts such nonsense. But the most sensible people consider it their duty to believe in a universal spirit!

120. All the gods, adored by men, are of savage origin. They have evidently been imagined by stupid people, or presented, by ambitious and crafty legislators, to

ignorant and uncivilized nations, who had neither capacity nor courage to examine the objects, which through terror they were made to worship.

By closely examining God, we are forced to acknowledge, that he evidently bears marks of a savage nature. To be savage is to acknowledge no right but force; it is to be cruel beyond measure; to follow only one's own caprice; to want foresight, prudence, and reason. Ye nations, who call yourselves civilized! Do you not discern, in this hideous character, the God, on whom you lavish your incense? Are not the descriptions given you of the divinity, visibly borrowed from the implacable, jealous, revengeful, sanguinary, capricious inconsiderate humour of man, who has not cultivated his reason? O men! You adore only a great savage, whom you regard, however, as a model to imitate, as an amiable master, as a sovereign full of perfection.

Religious opinions are ancient monuments of ignorance, credulity, cowardice, and barbarism of their ancestors. Every savage is a child fond of the marvellous, who believes every thing, and examines nothing. Ignorant of nature, he attributes to spirits, enchantments, and to magic, whatever appears to him extraordinary. His priests appear to him sorcerers, in whom he supposes a power purely divine, before whom his confounded reason humbles itself, whose oracles are to him infallible decrees which it would be dangerous to contradict.

In religion, men have, for the most part, remained in their primitive barbarity. Modern religions are only ancient follies revived, or presented under some new form. If the savages of antiquity adored mountains, rivers, serpents, trees, and idols of every kind; if the EGYPTIANS paid homage to crocodiles, rats, and onions, do we not see nations, who think themselves wiser than they, worship bread, into which they imagine, that through the enchantments of their priests, the divinity has descended. Is not the Bread-God the idol of many Christian nations, who, in this respect, are as irrational, as the most savage?

121. The ferocity, stupidity, and folly of uncivilized man have ever disclosed themselves in religious practices, either cruel or extravagant. A spirit of barbarity still survives, and penetrates the religions even of the most polished nations. Do we not still see human victims offered to the divinity? To appease the anger of a God, who is always supposed as ferocious, jealous and vindictive, as a savage, do not those, whose manner of thinking is supposed to displease him, expire under studied

torments, by the command of sanguinary laws? Modern nations, at the instigation of their priests, have perhaps improved upon the atrocious folly of barbarous nations; at least, we find, that it has ever entered the heads of savages to torment for opinions, to search the thoughts, to molest men for the invisible movements of their brains?

When we see learned nations, such as the English, French, German, etc., continue, notwithstanding their knowledge, to kneel before the barbarous God of the Jews; when we see these enlightened nations divide into sects, defame, hate, and despise one another for their equally ridiculous opinions concerning the conduct and intentions of this unreasonable God; when we see men of ability foolishly devote their time to meditate the will of this God, who is full of caprice and folly, we are tempted to cry out: O men, you are still savage!!!

122. Whoever has formed true ideas of the ignorance, credulity, negligence, and stupidity of the vulgar, will suspect opinions the more, as he finds them generally established. Men, for the most part, examine nothing: they blindly submit to custom and authority. Their religious opinions, above all others, are those which they have the least courage and capacity to examine: as they comprehend nothing about them, they are forced to be silent, or at least are soon destitute of arguments. Ask any man, whether he believes in a God? He will be much surprised that you can doubt it. Ask him again, what he understands by the word *God*. You throw him into the greatest embarrassment; you will perceive immediately, that he is incapable of affixing any real idea to this word, he incessantly repeats. He will tell you, that God is God. He knows neither what he thinks of it, nor his motives for believing in it.

All nations speak of a God; but do they agree upon this God? By no means. But division upon an opinion proves not its evidence; it is rather a sign of uncertainty and obscurity. Does the same man always agree with himself in the notions he forms of his God? No. His idea varies with the changes, which he experiences;-- another sign of uncertainty. Men always agree in demonstrative truths. In any situation, except that of insanity, every one knows that two and two make four, that the sun shines, that the whole is greater than its part; that benevolence is necessary to merit the affection of men; that injustice and cruelty are incompatible with goodness. Are they thus agreed when they speak of God? Whatever they think, or say of him, is immediately destroyed by the effects they attribute to him.

Ask several painters to represent a chimera, and each will paint it in a different manner. You will find no resemblance between the features, each has given it a portrait, that has no original. All theologians, in giving us a picture of God, give us one of a great chimera, in whose features they never agree, whom each arranges in his own way, and who exists only in their imaginations. There are not two individuals, who have, or can have, the same ideas of their God.

123. It might be said with more truth, that men are either skeptics or atheists, than that they are convinced of the existence of God. How can we be assured of the existence of a being, whom we could never examine, and of whom it is impossible to conceive any permanent idea? How can we convince ourselves of the existence of a being, to whom we are every moment forced to attribute conduct, opposed to the ideas, we had endeavoured to form of him? Is it then possible to believe what we cannot conceive? Is not such a belief the opinions of others without having any of our own? Priests govern by faith; but do not priests themselves acknowledge that God is to them incomprehensible? Confess then, that a full and entire conviction of the existence of God is not so general, as is imagined.

Scepticism arises from a want of motives sufficient to form a judgment. Upon examining the proofs which seem to establish, and the arguments which combat, the existence of God, some persons have doubted and withheld their assent. But this uncertainty arises from not having sufficiently examined. Is it possible to doubt any thing evident? Sensible people ridicule an absolute scepticism, and think it even impossible. A man, who doubted his own existence, or that of the sun, would appear ridiculous. Is this more extravagant than to doubt the non-existence of an evidently impossible being? Is it more absurd to doubt one's own existence, than to hesitate upon the impossibility of a being, whose qualities reciprocally destroy one another? Do we find greater probability for believing the existence of a spiritual being, than the existence of a stick without two ends? Is the notion of an infinitely good and powerful being, who causes or permits an infinity of evils, less absurd or impossible, than that of a square triangle? Let us conclude then, that religious scepticism can result only from a superficial examination of theological principles, which are in perpetual contradiction with the most clear and demonstrative principles.

To doubt, is to deliberate. Scepticism is only a state of indetermination, resulting from an insufficient examination of things. Is it possible for any one to be sceptical in matters of religion, who will deign to revert to its principles, and closely examine the notion of God, who serves as its basis? Doubt generally arises either from indolence, weakness, indifference, or incapacity. With many people, to doubt is to fear the trouble of examining things, which are thought uninteresting. But religion being presented to men as their most important concern in this and the future world, skepticism and doubt on this subject must occasion perpetual anxiety and must really constitute a bed of thorns. Every man who has not courage to contemplate, without prejudice, the God upon whom all religion is founded, can never know for what religion to decide: he knows not what he should believe or not believe, admit or reject, hope or fear.

Indifference upon religion must not be confounded with scepticism. This indifference is founded upon the absolute assurance, or at any rate upon the probable belief, that religion is not interesting. A persuasion that a thing which is pretended to be important is not so, or is only indifferent, supposes a sufficient examination of the thing, without which it would be impossible to have this persuasion. Those who call themselves sceptics in the fundamental points of religion, are commonly either indolent or incapable of examining.

124. In every country, we are assured, that a God has revealed himself. What has he taught men? Has he proved evidently that he exists? Has he informed them where he resides? Has he taught them what he is, or in what his essence consists? Has he clearly explained to them his intentions and plan? Does what he says of this plan correspond with the effects, which we see? No. He informs them solely, that *he is what he is*; that he is a *hidden God*; that his ways are unspeakable; that he is exasperated against all who have the temerity to fathom his decrees, or to consult reason in judging him or his works.

Does the revealed conduct of God answer the magnificent ideas which theologians would give us of his wisdom, goodness, justice, and omnipotence? By no means. In every revelation, this conduct announces a partial and capricious being, the protector of favourite people, and the enemy of all others. If he deigns to appear to some men, he takes care to keep all others in an invincible ignorance of his divine intentions. Every private revelation evidently announces in God, injustice, partiality and malignity.

Do the commands, revealed by any God, astonish us by their sublime reason or wisdom? Do they evidently tend to promote the happiness of the people, to whom the Divinity discloses them? Upon examining the divine commands, one sees in every country, nothing but strange ordinances, ridiculous precepts, impertinent ceremonies, puerile customs, oblations, sacrifices, and expiations, useful indeed to the ministers of God, but very burthensome to the rest of the citizens. I see likewise, that these laws often tend to make men unsociable, disdainful, intolerant, quarrelsome, unjust, and inhuman, to those who have not received the same revelations, the same ordinances, or the same favours from heaven.

125. Are the precepts of morality, announced by the Deity, really divine, or superior to those which every reasonable man might imagine? They are divine solely because it is impossible for the human mind to discover their utility. They make virtue consist in a total renunciation of nature, in a voluntary forgetfulness of reason, a holy hatred of ourselves. Finally, these sublime precepts often exhibit perfection in a conduct, cruel to ourselves, and perfectly useless to others.

Has a God appeared? Has he himself promulgated his laws? Has he spoken to men with his own mouth? I am told, that God has not appeared to a whole people; but that he has always manifested himself through the medium of some favourite personages, who have been intrusted with the care of announcing and explaining his intentions. The people have never been permitted to enter the sanctuary; the ministers of the gods have alone had the right to relate what passes there.

126. If in every system of divine revelation, I complain of not seeing either the wisdom, goodness, or equity of God; if I suspect knavery, ambition, or interest; it is replied, that God has confirmed by miracles the mission of those, who speak in his name. But was it not more simple for him to appear in person, to explain his nature and will? Again, if I have the curiosity to examine these miracles, I find, that they are improbable tales, related by suspected people, who had the greatest interest in giving out that they were the messengers of the Most High.

What witnesses are appealed to in order to induce us to believe incredible miracles? Weak people, who existed thousands of years ago, and who, even though they could attest these miracles, may be suspected of being duped by their own imagination, and imposed upon by the tricks of dexterous impostors. But, you will say, these miracles are written in books, which by tradition have been transmitted to us. By whom were these books written? Who are the men who have transmitted them? They are either the founders of religions themselves, or their adherents and assigns. Thus, in religion, the evidence of interested parties becomes irrefragable and incontestable.

127. God has spoken differently to every people. The Indian believes not a word of what He has revealed to the Chinese; the Mahometan considers as fables what He has said to the Christian; the Jew regards both the Mahometan and Christian as sacrilegious corrupters of the sacred law, which his God had given to his fathers. The Christian, proud of his more modern revelation, indiscriminately damns the Indian, Chinese, Mahometan, and even the Jew, from whom he receives his sacred books. Who is wrong or right? Each exclaims, *I am in the right!* Each adduces the same proofs: each mentions his miracles, diviners, prophets, and martyrs. The man of sense tells them, they are all delirious; that God has not spoken, if it is true that he is a spirit, and can have neither mouth nor tongue; that without borrowing the organ of mortals, God could inspire his creatures with what he would have them learn; and that, as they are all equally ignorant what to think of God, it is evident that it has not been the will of God to inform them on the subject.

The followers of different forms of worship which are established, accuse one another of superstition and impiety. Christians look with abhorrence upon the Pagan, Chinese, and Mahometan superstition. Roman Catholics treat, as impious, Protestant Christians; and the latter incessantly declaim against the superstition of the Catholics. They are all right. To be impious, is to have opinions offensive to the God adored; to be superstitious, is to have of him false ideas. In accusing one another of superstition, the different religionists resemble humpbacks, who reproach one another with their deformity.

128. Are the oracles, which the Divinity has revealed by his different messengers, remarkable for clearness? Alas! no two men interpret them alike. Those who explain them to others are not agreed among themselves. To elucidate them, they have recourse to interpretations, to commentaries, to allegories, to explanations: they discover *mystical sense* very different from the *literal sense*. Men are every where wanted to explain the commands of a God, who could not, or would not, announce himself clearly to those, whom he wished to enlighten.

129. The founders of religion, have generally proved their missions by miracles.

But what is a miracle? It is an operation directly opposite to the laws of nature. But who, according to you, made those laws? God. Thus, your God, who, according to you, foresaw every thing, counteracts the laws, which his wisdom prescribed to nature! These laws were then defective, or at least in certain circumstances they did not accord with the views of the same God, since you inform us that he judged it necessary to suspend or counteract them.

It is said, that a few men, favoured by the Most High, have received power to perform miracles. But to perform a miracle, it is necessary to have ability to create new causes capable of producing effects contrary to those of common causes. Is it easy to conceive, that God can give men the inconceivable power of creating causes out of nothing? Is it credible, that an immutable God can communicate to men power to change or rectify his plan, a power, which by his essence an immutable being cannot save himself? Miracles, far from doing much honour to God, far from proving the divinity of a religion, evidently annihilate the God idea. How can a theologian tell us, that God, who must have embraced the whole of his plan, who could have made none but perfect laws, and who cannot alter them, is forced to employ miracles to accomplish his projects, or can grant his creatures the power of working prodigies to execute his divine will? An omnipotent being, whose will is always fulfilled, who holds in his hand his creatures, has only to *will*, to make them believe whatever he desires.

130. What shall we say of religions that prove their divinity by miracles? How can we credit miracles recorded in the sacred books of the Christians, where God boasts of hardening the hearts and blinding those whom he wishes to destroy; where he permits malicious spirits and magicians to work miracles as great as those of his servants; where it is predicted, that *Antichrist* shall have power to perform prodigies capable of shaking the faith even of the elect? In this case, by what signs shall we know whether God means to instruct or ensnare us? How shall we distinguish whether the wonders, we behold, come from God or devil? To remove our perplexity, Pascal gravely tells us, that *it is necessary to judge the doctrine by the miracles, and the miracles by the doctrine; that the doctrine proves the miracles, and the miracles the doctrine*. If there exist a vicious and ridiculous circle, it is undoubtedly in this splendid reasoning of one of the greatest defenders of Christianity. Where is the religion, that does not boast of the most admirable doctrine, and which does not produce numerous

miracles for its support?

Is a miracle capable of annihilating the evidence of a demonstrated truth? Although a man should have the secret of healing all the sick, of making all the lame to walk, of raising in all the dead of a city, of ascending into the air, of stopping the course of the sun and moon, can he thereby convince me, that two and two do not make four, that one makes three, and that three make only one; that a God, whose immensity fills the universe, could have been contained in the body of a Jew; that the ETERNAL can die like a man; that a God, who is said to be immutable, provident, and sensible, could have changed his mind upon his religion, and reformed his own work by a new revelation?

131. According to the very principles either of natural or revealed theology, every new revelation should be regarded as false; every change in a religion emanated from the Deity should be reputed an impiety and blasphemy. Does not all reform suppose, that, in his first effort, God could not give his religion the solidity and perfection required? To say, that God, in giving a first law, conformed to the rude ideas of the people whom he wished to enlighten, is to pretend that God was neither able nor willing to render the people, whom he was enlightening, so reasonable as was necessary in order to please him.

Christianity is an impiety, if it is true that Judaism is a religion which has really emanated from a holy, immutable, omnipotent, and foreseeing God. The religion of Christ supposes either defects in the law which God himself had given by Moses, or impotence or malice in the same God, who was either unable or unwilling to render the Jews such as they ought to have been in order to please him. Every new religion, or reform of ancient religions, is evidently founded upon the impotence, inconstancy, imprudence, or malice of the Divinity.

132. If history informs me, that the first apostles, the founders or reformers of religions, wrought great miracles; history also informs me, that these reformers and their adherents were commonly buffeted, persecuted, and put to death, as disturbers of the peace of nations. I am therefore tempted to believe, that they did not perform the miracles ascribed to them; indeed, such miracles must have gained them numerous partisans among the eye-witnesses, who ought to have protected the operators from abuse. My incredulity redoubles, when I am told, that the workers of miracles were cruelly tormented, or ignominiously executed. How is it possible to

believe, that missionaries, protected by God, invested with his divine power, and enjoying the gift of miracles, could not have wrought such a simple miracle, as to escape the cruelty of their persecutors?

Priests have the art of drawing from the persecutions themselves, a convincing proof in favour of the religion of the persecuted. But a religion, which boasts of having cost the lives of many martyrs, and informs us, that its founders, in order to extend it, have suffered punishments, cannot be the religion of a beneficent, equitable and omnipotent God. A good God would not permit men, intrusted with announcing his commands, to be ill-treated. An all-powerful God, wishing to found a religion, would proceed in a manner more simple and less fatal to the most faithful of his servants. To say that God would have his religion sealed with blood, is to say that he is weak, unjust, ungrateful, and sanguinary; and that he is cruel enough to sacrifice his messengers to the views of his ambition.

133. To die for religion proves not that the religion is true, or divine; it proves, at most, that it is supposed to be such. An enthusiast proves nothing by his death, unless that religious fanaticism is often stronger than the love of life. An impostor may sometimes die with courage; he then makes, in the language of the proverb, *a virtue of necessity*.

People are often surprised and affected at sight of the generous courage and disinterested zeal, which has prompted missionaries to preach their doctrine, even at the risk of suffering the most rigorous treatment. From this ardour for the salvation of men, are drawn inferences favourable to the religion they have announced. But in reality, this disinterestedness is only apparent. He, who ventures nothing should gain nothing. A missionary seeks to make his fortune by his doctrine. He knows that, if he is fortunate enough to sell his commodity, he will become absolute master of those who receive him for their guide; he is sure of becoming the object of their attention, respect, and veneration. Such are the true motives, which kindle the zeal and charity of so many preachers and missionaries.

To die for an opinion, proves the truth or goodness of that opinion no more than to die in battle proves the justice of a cause, in which thousands have the folly to devote their lives. The courage of a martyr, elated with the idea of paradise, is not more supernatural, than the courage of a soldier, intoxicated with the idea of glory, or impelled by the fear of disgrace. What is the difference between an Iroquois, who sings while he is burning by inches, and the martyr ST. LAURENCE, who upon the gridiron insults his tyrant?

The preachers of a new doctrine fail, because they are the weakest; apostles generally practise a perilous trade. Their courageous death proves neither the truth of their principles nor their own sincerity, any more than the violent death of the ambitious man, or of the robber, proves, that they were right in disturbing society, or that they thought themselves authorised in so doing. The trade of a missionary was always flattering to ambition, and formed a convenient method of living at the expense of the vulgar. These advantages have often been enough to efface every idea of danger.

134. You tell us, theologians! that *what is folly in the eyes of men, is wisdom before God, who delights to confound the wisdom of the wise*. But do you not say, that human wisdom is a gift of heaven? In saying this wisdom displeases God, is but folly in his sight, and that he is pleased to confound it, you declare that your God is the friend only of ignorant people, and that he makes sensible people a fatal present for which this perfidious tyrant promises to punish them cruelly at some future day. Is it not strange, that one can be the friend of your God, only by declaring one's self the enemy of reason and good sense?

135. According to the divines, *faith is an assent without evidence*. Whence it follows, that religion requires us firmly to believe inevident things, and propositions often improbable or contrary to reason. But when we reject reason as a judge of faith, do we not confess, that reason is incompatible with faith? As the ministers of religion have resolved to banish reason, they must have felt the impossibility of reconciling it with faith, which is visibly only a blind submission to priests, whose authority seems to many persons more weighty than evidence itself, and preferable to the testimony of the senses.

"Sacrifice your reason; renounce experience; mistrust the testimony of your senses; submit without enquiry to what we announce to you in the name of heaven." Such is the uniform language of priests throughout the world; they agree upon no point, except upon the necessity of never reasoning upon the principles which they present to us as most important to our felicity!

I will *not* sacrifice my reason; because this reason alone enables me to distinguish good from evil, truth from falsehood. If, as you say, my reason comes from

God, I shall never believe that a God, whom you call good, has given me reason, as a snare, to lead me to perdition. Priests! do you not see, that, by decrying reason, you calumniate your God, from whom you declare it to be a gift.

I will *not* renounce experience; because it is a guide much more sure than the imagination or authority of spiritual guides. Experience teaches me, that enthusiasm and interest may blind and lead them astray themselves; and that the authority of experience ought to have much more influence upon my mind, than the suspicious testimony of many men, who I know are either very liable to be deceived themselves, or otherwise are very much interested in deceiving others.

I *will* mistrust my senses; because I am sensible they sometimes mislead me. But, on the other hand, I know that they will not always deceive me. I well know, that the eye shews me the sun much smaller than it really is; but experience, which is only the repeated application of the senses, informs me, that objects always appear to diminish, as their distance increases; thus I attain to a certainty, that the sun is much larger than the earth; thus my senses suffice to rectify the hasty judgments, which they themselves had caused.

In warning us to mistrust the testimony of our senses, the priests annihilate the proofs of all religion. If men may be dupes of their imagination; if their senses are deceitful, how shall we believe the miracles, which struck the treacherous senses of our ancestors? If my senses are unfaithful guides, I ought not to credit even the miracles wrought before my eyes.

136. You incessantly repeat that *the truths of religion are above reason*. If so, do you not perceive, that these truths are not adapted to reasonable beings? To pretend that reason can deceive us, is to say, that truth can be false; that the useful can be hurtful. Is reason any thing but a knowledge of the useful and true? Besides, as our reason and senses are our only guides in this life, to say they are unfaithful, is to say, that our errors are necessary, our ignorance invincible, and that, without the extreme of injustice, God cannot punish us for following the only guides it was his supreme will to give.

To say, we are obliged to believe things above our reason, is ridiculous. To assure us, that upon some objects we are not allowed to consult reason, is to say, that, in the most interesting matter, we must consult only imagination, or act only at random. Our divines say, we must sacrifice our reason to God. But what motives can we have to sacrifice our reason to a being, who makes us only useless presents, which he does not intend us to use? What confidence can we put in a God, who, according to our divines themselves, is malicious enough to harden the heart, to strike with blindness, to lay snares for us, to *lead us into temptation?* In fine, what confidence can we put in the ministers of this God, who, to guide us more conveniently, commands us to shut our eyes?

137. Men are persuaded, that religion is to them of all things the most serious, while it is precisely what they least examine for themselves. In pursuit of an office, a piece of land, a house, a place of profit; in any transaction or contract whatever, every one carefully examines all, takes the greatest precaution, weighs every word of a writing, is guarded against every surprise. Not so in religion; every one receives it at a venture, and believes it upon the word of others, without ever taking the trouble to examine.

Two causes concur to foster the negligence and carelessness of men, with regard to their religious opinions. The first is the despair of overcoming the obscurity, in which all religion is necessarily enveloped. Their first principles are only adapted to disgust lazy minds, who regard them as a chaos impossible to be understood. The second cause is, that every one is averse to being too much bound by severe precepts, which all admire in theory, but very few care to practice with rigour. The religion of many people is like old family ties, which they have never taken pains to examine, but which they deposit in their archives to have recourse to them occasionally.

138. The disciples of Pythagoras paid implicit faith to the doctrine of their master; *he has said it*, was to them the solution of every problem. The generality of men are not more rational. In matters of religion, a curate, a priest, an ignorant monk becomes master of the thoughts. Faith relieves the weakness of the human mind, to which application is commonly painful; it is much more convenient to depend upon others, than to examine for one's self. Inquiry, being slow and difficult, equally, displeases the stupidity of the ignorant, and the ardour of the enlightened. Such is undoubtedly the reason why Faith has so many partisans.

The more men are deficient in knowledge and reason, the more zealous they are in religion. In theological quarrels, the populace, like ferocious beasts, fall upon all those, against whom their priest is desirous of exciting them. A profound ignorance, boundless credulity, weak intellect, and warm imagination, are the materials, of which are made bigots, zealots, fanatics, and saints. How can the voice of reason be heard by them who make it a principle never to examine for themselves, but to submit blindly to the guidance of others? The saints and the populace are, in the hands of their directors, automatons, moved at pleasure.

139. Religion is an affair of custom and fashion. *We must do as others do.* But, among the numerous religions in the world, which should men choose? This inquiry would be too painful and long. They must therefore adhere to the religion of their fathers, to that of their country, which, having force on its side, must be the best.

If we judge of the intentions of Providence by the events and revolutions of this world, we are compelled to believe, that He is very indifferent about the various religions upon earth. For thousands of years, paganism, polytheism, idolatry, were the prevailing religions. We are now assured, that the most flourishing nations had not the least idea of God; an idea, regarded as so essential to the happiness of man. Christians say, all mankind lived in the grossest ignorance of their duties towards God, and had no notions of him, but what were insulting to his Divine Majesty. Christianity, growing out of Judaism, very humble in its obscure origin, became powerful and cruel under the Christian emperors, who, prompted by holy zeal, rapidly spread it in their empire by means of fire and sword, and established it upon the ruins of paganism. Mahomet and his successors, seconded by Providence or their victorious arms, in a short time banished the Christian religion from a part of Asia, Africa, and even Europe; and the *gospel* was then forced to yield to the *Koran*.

In all the factions or sects, which, for many ages have distracted Christianity, *the best argument has been always that of the strongest party*; arms have decided which doctrine is most conducive to the happiness of nations. May we not hence infer, either that the Deity feels little interested in the religion of men, or that he always declares in favour of the opinions, which best suit the interest of earthly powers; in fine, that he changes his plan to accommodate their fancy?

Rulers infallibly decide the religion of the people. The true religion is always the religion of the prince; the true God is the God, whom the prince desires his people to adore; the will of the priests, who govern the prince, always becomes the will of God. A wit justly observed, that *the true religion is always that, on whose side are the prince and the hangman.* Emperors and hangmen long supported the gods of Rome against the God of Christians; the latter, having gained to his interest the emperors, their soldiers, and their hangmen, succeeded in destroying the worship of the Roman gods. The God of Mahomet has dispossessed the God of Christians of a great part of the dominions, which he formerly occupied.

In the eastern part of Asia, is a vast, flourishing, fertile, populous country, governed by such wise laws, that the fiercest conquerors have adopted them with respect. I mean China. Excepting Christianity, which was banished as dangerous, the people there follow such superstitions as they please, while the *mandarins*, or magistrates, having long known the errors of the popular religion, are vigilant to prevent the *bonzes* or priests from using it as an instrument of discord. Yet we see not, that Providence refuses his blessing to a nation, whose chiefs are so indifferent about the worship that is rendered to him. On the contrary, the Chinese enjoy a happiness and repose worthy to be envied, by the many nations whom religion divides, and often devastates.

We cannot reasonably propose to divest the people of their follies; but we may perhaps cure the follies of those who govern the people, and who will then prevent the follies of the people from becoming dangerous. Superstition is to be feared only when princes and soldiers rally round her standard; then she becomes cruel and sanguinary. Every sovereign, who is the protector of one sect or religious faction, is commonly the tyrant of others, and becomes himself the most cruel disturber of the peace of his dominions.

140. It is incessantly repeated, and many sensible persons are induced to believe, that religion is a restraint necessary to men; that without it, there would no longer exist the least check for the vulgar; and that morality and religion are intimately connected with it. "The fear of the Lord," cries the priest, "is the beginning of wisdom. The terrors of another life are *salutary*, and are proper to curb the passions of men."

To perceive the inutility of religious notions, we have only to open our eyes and contemplate the morals of those nations, who are the most under the dominion of religion. We there find proud tyrants, oppressive ministers, perfidious courtiers, shameless extortioners, corrupt magistrates, knaves, adulterers, debauchees, prostitutes, thieves, and rogues of every kind, who have never doubted either the existence of an avenging and rewarding God, the torments of hell, or the joys of paradise. Without the least utility to the greater part of mankind, the ministers of religion have studied to render death terrible to the eyes of their followers. If devout Christians could but be consistent, they would pass their whole life in tears, and die under the most dreadful apprehensions. What can be more terrible than death, to the unfortunate who are told, *that it is horrible to fall into the hands of the living God; that we must work out our salvation with fear and trembling!* Yet we are assured, that the death of the Christian is attended with infinite consolations, of which the unbeliever is deprived. The good Christian, it is said, dies in the firm hope of an eternal happiness which he has strived to merit. But is not this firm assurance itself a presumption punishable in the eyes of a severe God? Ought not the greatest saints to be ignorant whether they are *worthy of love or hatred?* Ye Priests! while consoling us with the hope of the joys of paradise; have you then had the advantage to see your names and ours inscribed *in the book of life?*

141. To oppose the passions and present interests of men the obscure notions of a metaphysical, inconceivable God,--the incredible punishments of another life,--or the pleasures of the heaven, of which nobody has the least idea,--is not this combating realities with fictions? Men have never any but confused ideas of their God: they see him only in clouds. They never think of him when they are desirous to do evil: whenever ambition, fortune, or pleasure allures them, God's threatenings and promises are forgotten. In the things of this life, there is a degree of certainty, which the most lively faith cannot give to the things of another life.

Every religion was originally a curb invented by legislators, who wished to establish their authority over the minds of rude nations. Like nurses who frighten children to oblige them to be quiet, the ambitious used the name of the gods to frighten savages; and had recourse to terror in order to make them support quietly the yoke they wished to impose. Are then the bugbears of infancy made for riper age? At the age of maturity, no man longer believes them, or if he does, they excite little emotion in him, and never alter his conduct.

142. Almost every man fears what he sees much more than what he does not see; he fears the judgments of men of which he feels the effects, more than the judgments of God of whom he has only fluctuating ideas. The desire of pleasing the world, the force of custom, the fear of ridicule, and of censure, have more force

than all religious opinions. Does not the soldier, through fear of disgrace, daily expose his life in battle, even at the risk of incurring eternal damnation?

The most religious persons have often more respect for a varlet, than for God. A man who firmly believes, that God sees every thing, and that he is omniscient and omnipresent, will be guilty, when alone, of actions, which he would never do in presence of the meanest of mortals. Those, who pretend to be the most fully convinced of the existence of God, every moment act as if they believed the contrary.

143. "Let us, at least," it will be said, "cherish the idea of a God, which alone may serve as a barrier to the passions of kings." But, can we sincerely admire the wonderful effects, which the fear of this God generally produces upon the minds of princes, who are called his images? What idea shall we form of the original, if we judge of it by the copies!

Sovereigns, it is true, call themselves the representatives of God, his vicegerents upon earth. But does the fear of a master, more powerful than they are, incline them seriously to study the welfare of the nations, whom Providence has intrusted to their care? Does the pretended terror, which ought to be inspired into them by the idea of an invisible judge, to whom alone they acknowledge themselves accountable for their actions, render them more equitable, more compassionate, more sparing of blood and treasure of their subjects, more temperate in their pleasures, more attentive to their duties? In fine, does this God, by whose authority kings reign, deter them from inflicting a thousand evils upon the people to whom they ought to act as guides, protectors, and fathers? Alas! If we survey the whole earth, we shall see men almost every where governed by tyrants, who use religion merely as an instrument to render more stupid the slaves, whom they overwhelm under the weight of their vices, or whom they sacrifice without mercy to their extravagancies.

Far from being a check upon the passions of kings, Religion, by its very principles, frees them from all restraint. It transforms them into divinities, whose caprice the people are never permitted to resist. While it gives up the reins to princes, and on their part breaks the bonds of the social compact, it endeavours to chain the minds and hands of their oppressed subjects. Is it then surprising, that the gods of the earth imagine every thing lawful for them, and regard their subjects only as instruments of their caprice or ambition?

In every country, Religion has represented the Monarch of nature as a cruel, fantastical, partial tyrant, whose caprice is law; the Monarch God, is but too faithfully imitated by his representatives upon earth. Religion seems every where invented solely to lull the people in the lap of slavery, in order that their masters may easily oppress them, or render them wretched with impunity.

144. To guard against the enterprises of a haughty pontiff who wished to reign over kings, to shelter their persons from the attempts of credulous nations excited by the priests, several European princes have pretended to hold their crowns and rights from God alone, and to be accountable only to him for their actions. After a long contest between the civil and spiritual power, the former at length triumphed; and the priests, forced to yield, acknowledged the divine right of kings and preached them to the people, reserving the liberty of changing their minds and of preaching revolt, whenever the divine rights of kings clashed with the divine rights of the clergy. It was always at the expense of nations, that peace was concluded between kings and priests; but the latter, in spite of treaties, always preserved their pretensions.

Tyrants and wicked princes, whose consciences continually reproach them with negligence or perversity, far from fearing their God, had rather deal with this invisible judge who never opposes any thing, or with his priests who are always condescending to the rulers of the earth, than with their own subjects. The people, reduced to despair, might probably *appeal* from the divine right of their chiefs. Men when oppressed to the last degree, sometimes become turbulent; and the divine rights of the tyrant are then forced to yield to the natural rights of the subjects.

It is cheaper dealing with gods than men. Kings are accountable for their actions to God alone; priests are accountable only to themselves. There is much reason to believe, that both are more confident of the indulgence of heaven, than of that of earth. It is much easier to escape the vengeance of gods who may be cheaply appeased, than the vengeance of men whose patience is exhausted.

"If you remove the fear of an invisible power, what restraint will you impose upon the passions of sovereigns?" Let them learn to reign; let them learn to be just; to respect the rights if the people; and to acknowledge the kindness of the nations, from whom they hold their greatness and power. Let them learn to fear men, and to submit to the laws of equity. Let nobody transgress these laws with impunity;

and let them be equally binding upon the powerful and the weak, the great and the small, the sovereign and the subjects.

The fear of gods, Religion, and the terrors of another life, are the metaphysical and supernatural bulwarks, opposed to the impetuous passions of princes! Are these bulwarks effectual? Let experience resolve the question. To oppose Religion to the wickedness of tyrants, is to wish, that vague, uncertain, unintelligible speculations may be stronger than propensities which every thing conspires daily to strengthen.

145. The immense service of religion to politics is incessantly boasted; but, a little reflection will convince us, that religious opinions equally blind both sovereigns and people, and never enlighten them upon their true duties or interests. Religion but too often forms licentious, immoral despots, obeyed by slaves, whom every thing obliges to conform to their views.

For want of having studied or known the true principles of administration, the objects and rights of social life, the real interests of men and their reciprocal duties, princes, in almost every country, have become licentious, absolute, and perverse; and their subjects abject, wicked, and unhappy. It was to avoid the trouble of studying these important objects, that recourse was had to chimeras, which, far from remedying any thing, have hitherto only multiplied the evils of mankind, and diverted them from whatever is most essential to their happiness.

Does not the unjust and cruel manner in which so many nations are governed, manifestly furnish one of the strongest proofs, not only of the small effect produced by the fear of another life, but also of the non-existence of a Providence, busied with the fate of the human race? If there existed a good God, should we not be forced to admit, that in this life he strangely neglects the greater part of mankind? It would seem, that this God has created nations only to be the sport of the passions and follies of his representatives upon earth.

146. By reading history with attention, we shall perceive that Christianity, at first weak and servile, established itself among the savage and free nations of Europe only intimating to their chiefs, that its religious principles favoured despotism and rendered them absolute. Consequently, we see barbarous princes suddenly converted; that is, we see them adopt, without examination, a system so favourable to their ambition, and use every art to induce their subjects to embrace it. If the

ministers of this religion have since often derogated from their favourite principles, it is because the theory influences the conduct of the ministers of the Lord, only when it suits their temporal interests.

Christianity boasts of procuring men a happiness unknown to preceding ages. It is true, the Greeks knew not the *divine rights* of tyrants or of the usurpers of the rights of their country. Under paganism, it never entered the head of any man to suppose, that it was against the will of heaven for a nation to defend themselves against a ferocious beast, who had the audacity to lay waste their possessions. The religion of the Christians was the first that screened tyrants from danger, by laying down as a principle that the people must renounce the legitimate defence of themselves. Thus Christian nations are deprived of the first law of nature, which orders man to resist evil, and to disarm whoever is preparing to destroy him! If the ministers of the church have often permitted the people to revolt for the interest of heaven, they have never permitted them to revolt for their own deliverance from real evils or known violences.

From heaven came the chains, that were used for fettering the minds of mortals. Why is the Mahometan every where a slave? Because his prophet enslaved him in the name of the Deity, as Moses had before subdued the Jews. In all parts of the earth, we see, that the first legislators were the first sovereigns and the first priests of the savages, to whom they gave laws.

Religion seems invented solely to exalt princes above their nations, and rivet the fetters of slavery. As soon as the people are too unhappy here below, priests are ready to silence them by threatening them with the anger of God. They are made to fix their eyes upon heaven, lest they should perceive the true causes of their misfortunes, and apply the remedies which nature presents.

147. By dint of repeating to men, that the earth is not their true country; that the present life is only a passage; that they are not made to be happy in this world; that their sovereigns hold their authority from God alone, and are accountable only to him for the abuse of it; that it is not lawful to resist them, etc., priests have eternized the misgovernment of kings and the misery of the people; the interests of nations have been basely sacrificed to their chiefs. The more we consider the dogmas and principles of religion, the more we shall be convinced, that their sole object is the advantage of tyrants and priests, without regard to that of societies.

To mask the impotence of its deaf gods, religion has persuaded mortals, that iniquities always kindle the wrath of heaven. People impute to themselves alone the disasters that daily befal them. If nations sometimes feel the strokes of convulsed nature, their bad governments are but too often the immediate and permanent causes, from whence proceed the continual calamities which they are forced to endure. Are not the ambition, negligence, vices, and oppressions of kings and nobles, generally the causes of scarcity, beggary, wars, pestilences, corrupt morals, and all the multiplied scourges which desolate the earth?

In fixing men's eyes continually upon heaven; in persuading them, that all their misfortunes are effects of divine anger; in providing none but ineffectual and futile means to put an end to their sufferings, we might justly conclude, that the only object of priests was to divert nations from thinking about the true sources of their misery, and thus to render it eternal. The ministers of religion conduct themselves almost like those indigent mothers, who, for want of bread, sing their starved children to sleep, or give them playthings to divert their thoughts from afflicting hunger.

Blinded by error from their very infancy, restrained by the invisible bonds of opinion, overcome by panic terrors, their faculties blunted by ignorance, how should the people know the true causes of their wretchedness? They imagine that they can avert it by invoking the gods. Alas! do they not see, that it is, in the name of these gods, that they are ordered to present their throats to the sword of their merciless tyrants, in whom they might find the obvious cause of the evils under which they groan, and for whom they cease not to implore, in vain, the assistance of heaven?

Ye credulous people! In your misfortunes, redouble your prayers, offerings, and sacrifices; throng to your temples; fast in sack-cloth and ashes; bathe yourselves in your own tears; and above all, completely ruin yourselves to enrich your gods! You will only enrich their priests. The gods of heaven will be propitious, only when the gods of the earth shall acknowledge themselves, men, like you, and shall devote to your welfare the attention you deserve.

148. Negligent, ambitious, and perverse Princes are the real causes of public misfortunes. Useless, unjust Wars depopulate the earth. Encroaching and despotic Governments absorb the benefits of nature. The rapacity of Courts discourages ag-

riculture, extinguishes industry, produces want, pestilence and misery. Heaven is neither cruel nor propitious to the prayers of the people; it is their proud chiefs, who have almost always hearts of stone.

It is destructive to the morals of princes, to persuade them that they have God alone to fear, when they injure their subjects, or neglect their happiness. Sovereigns! It is not the gods, but your people, that you offend, when you do evil. It is your people and yourselves that you injure, when you govern unjustly.

In history, nothing is more common than to see Religious Tyrants; nothing more rare than to find equitable, vigilant, enlightened princes. A monarch may be pious, punctual in a servile discharge of the duties of his religion, very submissive and liberal to his priests, and yet at the same time be destitute of every virtue and talent necessary for governing. To princes, Religion is only an instrument destined to keep the people more completely under the yoke. By the excellent principles of religious morality, a tyrant who, during a long reign, has done nothing but oppress his subjects, wresting, from them the fruits of their labour, sacrificing them without mercy to his insatiable ambition,--a conqueror, who has usurped the provinces of others, slaughtered whole nations, and who, during his whole life, has been a scourge to mankind,--imagines his conscience may rest, when, to expiate so many crimes, he has wept at the feet of a priest, who generally has the base complaisance to console and encourage a robber, whom the most hideous despair would too lightly punish for the misery he has caused upon earth.

149. A sovereign, sincerely devout, is commonly dangerous to the state. Credulity always supposes a contracted mind; devotion generally absorbs the attention, which a prince should pay to the government of his people. Obsequious to the suggestions of his priests, he becomes the sport of their caprices, the favourer of their quarrels, and the instrument and accomplice of their follies, which he imagines to be of the greatest importance. Among the most fatal presents, which religion has made the world, ought to be reckoned those devout and zealous monarchs, who, under an idea of working for the welfare of their subjects, have made it a sacred duty to torment, persecute, and destroy those, who thought differently from themselves. A bigot, at the head of an empire, is one of the greatest scourges. A single fanatical or knavish priest, listened to by a credulous and powerful prince, suffices to put a state in disorder.

In almost all countries, priests and pious persons are intrusted with forming the minds and hearts of young princes, destined to govern nations. What qualifications have instructors of this stamp! By what interests can they be animated? Full of prejudices themselves, they will teach their pupil to regard superstition, as most important and sacred; its chimerical duties, as most indispensable, intolerance and persecution, as the true foundation of his future authority. They will endeavour to make him a party leader, a turbulent fanatic, a tyrant; they will early stifle his reason, and forewarn him against the use of it; they will prevent truth from reaching his ears; they will exasperate him against true talents, and prejudice him in favour of contemptible ones; in short, they will make him a weak devotee, who will have no idea either of justice or injustice, nor of true glory, nor of true greatness, and who will be destitute of the knowledge and virtues necessary to the government of a great nation. Such is the plan of the education of a child, destined one day to create the happiness or misery of millions of men!

150. Priests have ever shewn themselves the friends of despotism, and the enemies of public liberty: their trade requires abject and submissive slaves, who have never the audacity to reason. In an absolute government, who ever gains an ascendancy over the mind of a weak and stupid prince, becomes master of the state. Instead of conducting the people to salvation, priests have always conducted them to servitude.

In consideration of the supernatural titles, which religion has forged for the worst of princes, the latter have commonly united with priests, who, sure of governing by opinion the sovereign himself, have undertaken to bind the hands of the people and to hold them under the yoke. But the tyrant, covered with the shield of religion, in vain flatters himself that he is secure from every stroke of fate; opinion is a weak rampart against the despair of the people. Besides, the priest is a friend of the tyrant only while he finds his account in tyranny; he preaches sedition, and demolishes the idol he has made, when he finds it no longer sufficiently conformable to the interest of God, whom he makes to speak at his will, and who never speaks except according to his interests.

It will no doubt be said, that sovereigns, knowing all the advantages which religion procures them, are truly interested in supporting it with all their strength. If religious opinions are useful to tyrants, it is very evident, that they are useful to those, who govern by the laws of reason and equity. Is there then any advantage in exercising tyranny? Are princes truly interested in being tyrants? Does not tyranny deprive them of true power, of the love of the people, and of all safety? Ought not every reasonable prince to perceive, that the despot is a madman, and an enemy to himself? Should not every enlightened prince beware of flatterers, whose object is to lull him to sleep upon the brink of the precipice which they form beneath him?

151. If sacerdotal flatteries succeed in perverting princes and making them tyrants; tyrants, on their part, necessarily corrupt both the great and the humble. Under an unjust ruler, void of goodness and virtue, who knows no law but his caprice, a nation must necessarily be depraved. Will this ruler wish to have, about his person, honest, enlightened, and virtuous men? No. He wants none but flatterers, approvers, imitators, slaves, base and servile souls, who conform themselves to his inclinations. His court will propagate the contagion of vice among the lower ranks. All will gradually become corrupted in a state, whose chief is corrupt. It was long since said, that "Princes seem to command others to do whatever they do themselves."

Religion, far from being a restraint upon sovereigns, enables them to indulge without fear or remorse, in acts of licentiousness as injurious to themselves, as to the nations whom they govern. It is never with impunity, that men are deceived. Tell a sovereign, that he is a god; he will very soon believe that he owes nothing to any one. Provided he is feared, he will care very little about being loved: he will observe neither rules, nor relations with his subjects, nor duties towards them. Tell this prince, that he is *accountable for his actions to God alone*, and he will soon act as if he were accountable to no one.

152. An enlightened sovereign is he, who knows his true interests; who knows, that they are connected with the interests of his nation; that a prince cannot be great, powerful, beloved, or respected, while he commands only unhappy slaves; that equity, beneficence, and vigilance will give him more real authority over his people, than the fabulous titles, said to be derived from heaven. He will see, that Religion is useful only to priests, that it is useless to society and often troubles it, and that it ought to be restrained in order to be prevented from doing injury. Finally, he will perceive, that, to reign with glory, he must have good laws and inculcate virtue, and not found his power upon impostures and fallacies.

153. The ministers of religion have taken great care to make of their God, a formidable, capricious, and fickle tyrant. Such a God was necessary to their variable interests. A God, who should be just and good, without mixture of caprice or perversity; a God, who had constantly the qualities of an honest man, or of a kind sovereign, would by no means suit his ministers. It is useful to priests, that men should tremble before their God, in order that they may apply to them to obtain relief from their fears. "No man is a hero before his valet de chambre." It is not surprising, that a God, dressed up by his priests so as to be terrible to others, should rarely impose upon them, or should have but very little influence upon their conduct. Hence, in every country, their conduct is very much the same. Under pretext of the glory of their God, they every where prey upon ignorance, degrade the mind, discourage industry, and sow discord. Ambition and avarice have at all times been the ruling passions of the priesthood. The priest every where rises superior to sovereigns and laws; we see him every where occupied with the interests of his pride, of his cupidity, and of his despotic, revengeful humour. In the room of useful and social virtues, he everywhere substitutes expiations, sacrifices, ceremonies, mysterious practices, in a word, inventions lucrative to himself and ruinous to others.

The mind is confounded and the reason is amazed upon viewing the ridiculous customs and pitiful means, which the ministers of the gods have invented in every country to purify souls, and render heaven favourable. Here they cut off part of a child's prepuce, to secure for him divine benevolence; there, they pour water upon his head, to cleanse him of crimes, which he could not as yet have committed. In one place, they command him to plunge into a river, whose waters have the power of washing away all stains; in another, he is forbidden to eat certain food, the use of which will not fail to excite the celestial wrath; in other countries, they enjoin upon sinful man to come periodically and confess his faults to a priest, who is often a greater sinner than himself, etc., etc., etc.

154. What should we say of a set of empirics, who, resorting every day to a public place, should extol the goodness of their remedies, and vend them as infallible, while they themselves were full of the infirmities, which they pretend to cure? Should we have much confidence in the recipes of these quacks, though they stun us with crying, "take our remedies, their effects are infallible; they cure every body; except us." What should we afterwards think, should those quacks spend

their lives in complaining, that their remedies never produced the desired effect upon the sick, who take them? In fine, what idea should we form of the stupidity of the vulgar, who, notwithstanding these confessions, should not cease to pay dearly for remedies, the inefficacy of which every thing tends to prove? Priests resemble these alchymists, who boldly tell us, they have the secret of making gold, while they have scarcely clothes to cover their nakedness.

The ministers of religion incessantly declaim against the corruption of the age, and loudly complain of the little effect of their lessons, while at the same time they assure us, that religion is the *universal remedy*, the true *panacea* against the wickedness of mankind. These priests are very sick themselves, yet men continue to frequent their shops, and to have faith in their divine antidotes, which, by their own confession, never effect a cure!

155. Religion, especially with the moderns, has tried to identify itself with Morality, the principles of which it has thereby totally obscured. It has rendered men unsociable by duty, and forced them to be inhuman to everyone who thought differently from themselves. Theological disputes, equally unintelligible to each of the enraged parties, have shaken empires, caused revolutions, been fatal to sovereigns, and desolated all Europe. These contemptible quarrels have not been extinguished even in rivers of blood. Since the extinction of paganism, the people have made it a religious principle to become outrageous, whenever any opinion is advanced which their priests think contrary to *sound doctrine*. The sectaries of a religion, which preaches, in appearance, nothing but charity, concord, and peace, have proved themselves more ferocious than cannibals or savages, whenever their divines excited them to destroy their brethren. There is no crime, which men have not committed under the idea of pleasing the Divinity, or appeasing his wrath.

The idea of a terrible God, whom we paint to ourselves as a despot, must necessarily render his subjects wicked. Fear makes only slaves, and slaves are cowardly, base, cruel, and think every thing lawful, in order to gain the favour or escape the chastisements of the master whom they fear. Liberty of thinking alone can give men humanity and greatness of soul. The notion of a tyrant-god tends only to make them abject, morose, quarrelsome, intolerant slaves.

Every religion, which supposes a God easily provoked, jealous, revengeful, punctilious about his rights or the etiquette with which he is treated;--a God little enough to be hurt by the opinions which men can form of him;--a God unjust enough to require that we have uniform notions of his conduct; a religion which supposes such a God necessarily becomes restless, unsociable, and sanguinary; the worshippers of such a God would never think, that they could, without offence, forbear hating and even destroying every one, who is pointed out to them, as an adversary of this God; they would think, that it would be to betray the cause of their celestial Monarch, to live in friendly intercourse with rebellious fellow-citizens. If we love what God hates, do we not expose ourselves to his implacable hatred?

Infamous persecutors, and devout men-haters! Will you never discern the folly and injustice of your intolerant disposition? Do you not see, that man is no more master of his religious opinions, his belief or unbelief, than of the language, which he learns from infancy? To punish a man for his errors, is it not to punish him for having been educated differently from you? If I am an unbeliever, is it possible for me to banish from my mind the reasons that have shaken my faith? If your God gives men leave to be damned, what have you to meddle with? Are you more prudent and wise, than this God, whose rights you would avenge?

156. There is no devotee, who does not, according to his temperament, hate, despise, or pity the adherents of a sect, different from his own. The *established* religion, which is never any other than that of the sovereign and the armies, always makes its superiority felt in a very cruel and injurious manner by the weaker sects. As yet there is no true toleration upon earth; men every where adore a jealous God, of whom each nation believes itself the friend, to the exclusion of all others.

Every sect boasts of adoring alone the true God, the universal God, the Sovereign of all nature. But when we come to examine this Monarch of the world, we find that every society, sect, party, or religious cabal, makes of this powerful God only a pitiful sovereign, whose care and goodness extend only to a small number of his subjects, who pretend that they alone have the happiness to enjoy his favours, and that he is not at all concerned about the others.

The founders of religions, and the priests who support them, evidently proposed to separate the nations, whom they taught, from the other nations; they wished to separate their own flock by distinguishing marks; they gave their followers gods, who were hostile to the other gods; they taught them modes of worship, dogmas and ceremonies apart; and above all, they persuaded them, that the religion of others was impious and abominable. By this unworthy artifice, the ambitious knaves established, their usurpation over the minds of their followers, rendered them unsociable, and made them regard with an evil eye all persons who had not the same mode of worship and the same ideas as they had. Thus it is, that Religion has shut up the heart and for ever banished from it the affection that man ought to have for his fellow-creature. Sociability, indulgence, humanity, those first virtues of all morality, are totally incompatible with religious prejudices.

157. Every national religion is calculated to make man vain, unsociable, and wicked; the first step towards humanity is to permit every one peaceably to embrace the mode of worship and opinions, which he judges to be right. But this conduct cannot be pleasing to the ministers of religion, who wish to have the right of tyrannizing over men even in their thoughts.

Blind and bigoted princes! You hate and persecute heretics, and order them to execution, because you are told, that these wretches displease God. But do you not say, that your God is full of goodness? How then can you expect to please him by acts of barbarity, which he must necessarily disapprove? Besides, who has informed you, that their opinions displease your God? Your priests? But, who assures you, that your priests are not themselves deceived or wish to deceive you? The same priests? Princes! It is then upon the hazardous word of your priests, that you commit the most atrocious crimes, under the idea of pleasing the Divinity!

158. Pascal says, "that man never does evil so fully and cheerfully, as when he acts from a false principle of conscience." Nothing is more dangerous than a religion, which lets loose the ferocity of the multitude, and justifies their blackest crimes. They will set no bounds to their wickedness, when they think it authorized by their God, whose interests, they are told, can make every action legitimate. Is religion in danger?--the most civilized people immediately becomes true savages, and think nothing forbidden. The more cruel they are, the more agreeable they suppose they are to their God, whose cause they imagine cannot be supported with too much warmth.

All religions have authorized innumerable crimes. The Jews, intoxicated with the promises of their God, arrogated the rights of exterminating whole nations. Relying on the oracles of their God, the Romans conquered and ravaged the world. The Arabians, encouraged by their divine prophet, carried fire and sword among the Christians and the idolaters.   The CHRISTIANS, under pretext of extending their holy religion, have often deluged both hemispheres in blood.

In all events favourable to their own interest, which they always call *the cause of God*, priests show us the *finger of God*. According to these principles, the devout have the happiness to see the *finger of God* in revolts, revolutions, massacres, regicides, crimes, prostitutions, horrors; and, if these things contribute ever so little to the triumph of religion, we are told, that "God uses all sorts of means to attain his ends." Is any thing more capable of effacing every idea of morality from the minds of men, than to inform them, that their God, so powerful and perfect, is often forced to make use of criminal actions in order to accomplish his designs?

159.   No sooner do we complain of the extravagancies and evils, which Religion has so often caused upon the earth, than we are reminded, that these excesses are not owing to Religion; but "that they are the sad effects of the passions of men." But I would ask, what has let loose these passions? It is evidently Religion; it is zeal, that renders men inhuman, and serves to conceal the greatest atrocities. Do not these disorders then prove, that religion, far from restraining the passions of men, only covers them with a veil, which sanctifies them, and that nothing would be more useful, than to tear away this sacred veil of which men often make such a terrible use? What horrors would be banished from society, if the wicked were deprived of so plausible a pretext for disturbing it!

Instead of being angels of peace among men, priests have been demons of discord. They have pretended to receive from heaven the right of being quarrelsome, turbulent, and rebellious. Do not the ministers of the Lord think themselves aggrieved, and pretend that the divine Majesty is offended, whenever sovereigns have the temerity to prevent them from doing evil? Priests are like the spiteful woman who cried *fire! murder! assassination!* while her husband held her hands to prevent her from striking him.

160.   Notwithstanding the bloody tragedies, which Religion often acts, it is insisted, that, without Religion, there can be no Morality. If we judge theological opinions by their effects, we may confidently assert, that all Morality is perfectly incompatible with men's religious opinions.

"Imitate God," exclaim the pious. But, what would be our Morality, should we imitate this God! and what God ought we to imitate? The God of the Deist? But even this God cannot serve us as a very constant model of goodness. If he is the author of all things, he is the author both of good and evil. If he is the author of order, he is also the author of disorder, which could not take place without his permission. If he produces, he destroys; if he gives life, he takes it away; if he grants abundance, riches, prosperity, and peace, he permits or sends scarcity, poverty, calamities, and wars. How then can we receive as a model of permanent beneficence, the God of Deism or natural religion, whose favourable dispositions are every instant contradicted by all the effects we behold? Morality must have a basis less tottering than the example of a God, whose conduct varies, and who cannot be called good, unless we obstinately shut our eyes against the evil which he causes or permits in this world.

Shall we imitate the *beneficent, mighty Jupiter* of heathen antiquity? To imitate such a god, is to admit as a model, a rebellious son, who ravishes the throne from his father. It is to imitate a debauchee, an adulterer, one guilty of incest and of base passions, at whose conduct every reasonable mortal would blush. What would have been the condition of men under paganism, had they imagined, like Plato, that virtue consisted in imitating the gods!

Must we imitate the God of the Jews! Shall we find in *Jehovah* a model for our conduct? This is a truly savage god, made for a stupid, cruel, and immoral people; he is always furious, breathes nothing but vengeance, commands carnage, theft, and unsociability. The conduct of this god cannot serve as a model to that of an honest man, and can be imitated only by a chief of robbers.

Shall we then imitate the *Jesus* of the Christians? Does this God, who died to appease the implacable fury of his father, furnish us an example which men ought to follow? Alas! we shall see in him only a God, or rather a fanatic, a misanthrope, who, himself plunged in wretchedness and preaching to wretches, will advise them to be poor, to combat with and stifle nature, to hate pleasure, seek grief, and detest themselves. He will tell them to leave father, mother, relations, friends, etc., to follow him. "Fine morality!" you say. It is, undoubtedly, admirable: it must be divine, for it is impracticable to men. But is not such sublime morality calculated to render virtue odious? According to the so much boasted morality of the *man*-God of the Christians, a disciple of his in this world must be like *Tantalus*, tormented with a burning thirst, which he is not allowed to quench. Does not such morality give us a wonderful idea of the author of nature? If, as we are assured, he has created all things for his creatures, by what strange whim does he forbid them the use of the goods he has created for them? Is pleasure then, which man continually desires, only a snare, which God has maliciously laid to surprise his weakness?

161. The followers of Christ would have us regard, as a miracle, the establishment of their Religion, which is totally repugnant to nature, opposite to all the propensities of the heart, and inimical to sensual pleasures. But the austerity of a doctrine renders it the more marvellous in the eyes of the vulgar. The same disposition, which respects inconceivable mysteries as divine and supernatural, admires, as divine and supernatural, a Morality, that is impracticable, and beyond the powers of man.

To admire a system of Morality, and to put it in practice, are two very different things. All Christians admire and extol the Morality of the gospel; which they do not practise.

The whole world is more or less infected with a Religious morality, founded upon the opinion, that to please the Divinity, it is absolutely necessary to render ourselves unhappy upon earth. In all parts of our globe, we see penitents, fakirs, and fanatics, who seem to have profoundly studied the means of tormenting themselves, in honour of a being whose goodness all agree in celebrating. Religion, by its essence, is an enemy to the joy and happiness of men. "Blessed are the poor, blessed are they, who weep; blessed are they, who suffer; misery to those, who are in abundance and joy." Such are the rare discoveries, announced by Christianity!

162. What is a Saint in every religion? A man, who prays, and fasts, who torments himself, and shuns the world; who like an owl, delights only in solitude, abstains from all pleasure, and seems frightened of every object, which may divert him from his fanatical meditations. Is this virtue? Is a being of this type, kind to himself, or useful to others? Would not society be dissolved, and man return to a savage state, if every one were fool enough to be a Saint?

It is evident, that the literal and rigorous practice of the divine Morality of the Christians would prove the infallible ruin of nations. A Christian, aiming at perfection, ought to free his mind from whatever can divert it from heaven, his true country. Upon earth, he sees nothing but temptations, snares, and rocks of perdition. He must fear science, as hurtful to faith; he must avoid industry, as a means of obtaining riches, too fatal to salvation; he must renounce offices and honours, as capable of exciting his pride, and calling off his attention from the care of his soul. In a word, the sublime Morality of Christ, were it practicable, would break all the bonds of society.

A Saint in society is as useless, as a Saint in the desert; his humour is morose, discontented, and often turbulent; his zeal sometimes obliges him in conscience to trouble society by opinions or dreams, which his vanity makes him consider as inspirations from on high. The annals of every religion are full of restless Saints, intractable Saints, and seditious Saints, who have become famous by the ravages, with which, *for the greater glory of God*, they have desolated the universe. If Saints, who live in retirement, are useless, those who live in the world, are often very dangerous.

The vanity of acting, the desire of appearing illustrious and peculiar in conduct, commonly constitute the distinguishing character of Saints. Pride persuades them, that they are extraordinary men far above human nature, beings much more perfect than others, favourites whom God regards with much more complaisance than the rest of mortals. Humility, in a Saint, is commonly only a more refined pride than that of the generality of men. Nothing but the most ridiculous vanity can induce man to wage continual war against his own nature.

163. A morality, which contradicts the nature of man, is not made for man. "But," say you, "the nature of man is depraved." In what consists this pretended depravity? In having passions? But, are not passions essential to man? Is he not obliged to seek, desire, and love what is, or what he thinks is, conducive to his happiness? Is he not forced to fear and avoid what he judges disagreeable or fatal? Kindle his passions for useful objects; connect his welfare with those objects; divert him, by sensible and known motives, from what may injure either him or others, and you will make him a reasonable and virtuous being. A man without passions would be equally indifferent to vice and to virtue.

Holy Doctors! you are always repeating to us that the nature of man is perverted; you exclaim, "that *all flesh has corrupted its way*, that all the propensities of nature have become inordinate." In this case, you accuse your God; who was either unable, or unwilling, that this nature should preserve its primitive perfection. If this nature is corrupted, why has not God repaired it? The Christian immediately assures me, "that human nature is repaired; that the death of his God has restored its integrity." How then, I would ask, do you pretend that human nature, notwithstanding the death of a God, is still depraved? Is then the death of your God wholly fruitless? What becomes of his omnipotence and of his victory over the Devil, if it is true that the Devil still preserves the empire, which, according to you, he has always exercised in the world?

According to Christian theology, Death is the *wages of sin*. This opinion is conformable to that of some negro and savage nations, who imagine that the Death of a man is always the supernatural effect of the anger of the Gods. Christians firmly believe, that Christ has delivered them from sin; though they see, that, in their Religion, as in others, man is subject to Death. To say that Jesus Christ has delivered us from sin, is it not to say, that a judge has pardoned a criminal, while we see that he leaves him for execution?

164. If shutting our eyes upon whatever passes in the world, we would credit the partisans of the Christian Religion, we should believe, that the coming of their divine Saviour produced the most wonderful and complete reform in the morals of nations.

If we examine the Morals of Christian nations, and listen to the clamours of their priests, we shall be forced to conclude, that Jesus Christ, their God, preached and died, in vain; his omnipotent will still finds in men, a resistance, over which he cannot, or will not triumph. The Morality of this divine Teacher, which his disciples so much admire and so little practise, is followed, in a whole century only by half a dozen obscure saints, and fanatics, and unknown monks, who alone will have the glory of shining in the celestial court, while all the rest of mortals, though redeemed by the blood of this God, will be the prey of eternal flames.

165. When a man is strongly inclined to sin, he thinks very little about his God. Nay more, whatever crimes he has committed, he always flatters himself, that this God will soften, in his favour, the rigour of his decrees. No mortal seriously believes, that his conduct can damn him. Though he fears a terrible God, who often makes him tremble, yet, whenever he is strongly tempted, he yields; and he afterwards sees only the God of *mercies*, the idea of whom calms his apprehensions. If a man commits evil, he hopes, he shall have time to reform, and promises to repent at a future day.

In religious pharmacy, there are infallible prescriptions to quiet consciences: priests, in every country, possess sovereign secrets to disarm the anger of heaven. Yet, if it be true that the Deity is appeased by prayers, offerings, sacrifices, and penances, it can no longer be said, that Religion is a check to the irregularities of men; they will first sin, and then seek the means to appease God. Every Religion, which expiates crime and promises a remission of them, if it restrain some persons, encourages the majority to commit evil. Notwithstanding his immutability, God, in every Religion, is a true *Proteus*. His priests represent him at one time armed with severity, at another full of clemency and mildness; sometimes cruel and unmerciful, and sometimes easily melted by the sorrow and tears of sinners. Consequently, men see the Divinity only on the side most conformable to their present interests. A God always angry would discourage his worshippers, or throw them into despair. Men must have a God, who is both irritable, and placable. If his anger frightens some timorous souls, his clemency encourages the resolutely wicked, who depend upon recurring, sooner or later, to the means of accommodation. If the judgments of God terrify some faint-hearted pious persons, who by constitution and habit are not prone to evil, *the treasures of divine mercy* encourage the greatest criminals, who have reason to hope they participate therein equally with the others.

166. Most men seldom think of God, or, at least, bestow on him serious attention. The only ideas we can form of him are so devoid of object, and are at the same time so afflicting, that the only imaginations they can arrest are those of melancholy hypochondriacs, who do not constitute the majority of the inhabitants of this world. The vulgar have no conception of God; their weak brains are confused, whenever they think of him. The man of business thinks only of his business; the courtier of his intrigues; men of fashion, women, and young people of their pleasures; dissipation soon effaces in them all the fatiguing notions of Religion. The ambitious man, the miser and the debauchee carefully avoid speculations too feeble to counterbalance their various passions.

Who is awed by the idea of a God? A few enfeebled men, morose and disgusted with the world; a few, in whom the passions are already deadened by age, by infirmity, or by the strokes of fortune. Religion is a check, to those alone who by their state of mind and body, or by fortuitous circumstances, have been already brought to reason. The fear of God hinders from sin only those, who are not much inclined to it, or else those who are no longer able to commit it. To tell men, that the Deity punishes crimes in this world, is to advance an assertion, which experience every moment contradicts. The worst of men are commonly the arbiters of the world, and are those whom fortune loads with her favours. To refer us to another life, in order to convince us of the judgments of God, is to refer us to conjectures, in order to destroy facts, which cannot be doubted.

167. Nobody thinks of the life to come, when he is strongly smitten with the objects he finds here below. In the eyes of a passionate lover, the presence of his mistress extinguishes the flames of hell, and her charms efface all the pleasures of paradise. Woman! you leave, say you, your lover for your God. This is either because your lover is no longer the same in your eyes, or because he leaves you.

Nothing is more common, than to see ambitious, perverse, corrupt, and immoral men, who have some ideas of Religion, and sometimes appear even zealous for its interest. If they do not practise it at present, they hope to in the future. They lay it up, as a remedy, which will be necessary to salve the conscience for the evil they intend to commit. Besides, the party of devotees and priests being very numerous, active, and powerful, is it not astonishing, that rogues and knaves seek its support to attain their ends? It will undoubtedly be said, that many honest people are sincerely religious, and that without profit; but is uprightness of heart always accompanied with knowledge?

It is urged, that many learned men, many men of genius have been strongly attached to Religion. This proves, that men of genius may have prejudices, be pusillanimous, and have an imagination, which misleads them and prevents them from examining subjects coolly. Pascal proves nothing in favour of Religion, unless that a man of genius may be foolish on some subjects, and is but a child, when he is weak enough to listen to his prejudices. Pascal himself tells us, that *the mind may be strong and contracted, enlarged and weak*. He previously observes, that *a man may have a sound mind, and not understand every subject equally well; for there are some, who, having a sound judgment in a certain order of things, are bewildered in others*.

168. What is virtue according to theology? *It is*, we are told, *the conformity of the actions of man to the will of God*. But, what is God? A being, of whom nobody has the least conception, and whom every one consequently modifies in his own way. What is the will of God? It is what men, who have seen God, or whom God has

inspired, have declared to be the will of God. Who are those, who have seen God? They are either fanatics, or rogues, or ambitious men, whom we cannot believe.

To found Morality upon a God, whom every man paints to himself differently, composes in his way, and arranges according to his own temperament and interest, is evidently to found Morality upon the caprice and imagination of men; it is to found it upon the whims of a sect, a faction, a party, who believe they have the advantage to adore a true God to the exclusion of all others.

To establish Morality or the duties of man upon the divine will, is to found it upon the will, the reveries and the interests of those, who make God speak, without ever fearing that he will contradict them. In every Religion, priests alone have a right to decide what is pleasing or displeasing to their God, and we are certain they will always decide, that it is what pleases or displeases themselves. The dogmas, the ceremonies, the morals, and the virtues, prescribed by every Religion, are visibly calculated only to extend the power or augment the emoluments of the founders and ministers of these Religions. The dogmas are obscure, inconceivable, frightful, and are therefore well calculated to bewilder the imagination and to render the vulgar more obsequious to the will of those who wish to domineer over them. The ceremonies and practices procure the priests, riches or respect. Religion consists in a submissive faith, which prohibits the exercise of reason; in a devout humility, which insures priests the submission of their slaves; in an ardent zeal, when Religion, that is, when the interest of these priests, is in danger. The only object of all religions is evidently the advantage of its ministers.

169. When we reproach theologians with the barrenness of their divine virtues, they emphatically extol *charity*, that tender love of one's neighbour, which Christianity makes an essential duty of its disciples. But, alas! what becomes of this pretended charity, when we examine the conduct of the ministers of the Lord? Ask them, whether we must love or do good to our neighbour, if he be an impious man, a heretic, or an infidel, that is, if he do not think like them? Ask them, whether we must tolerate opinions contrary to those of the religion, they profess? Ask them, whether the sovereign can show indulgence to those who are in error? Their charity instantly disappears, and the established clergy will tell you, that *the prince bears the sword only to support the cause of the Most High*: they will tell you that, through love for our neighbour, we must prosecute, imprison, exile, and burn him. You will find

no toleration except among a few priests, persecuted themselves, who will lay aside Christian charity the instant they have power to persecute in their turn.

The Christian religion, in its origin preached by beggars and miserable men, under the name of *charity*, strongly recommends alms. The religion of Mahomet also enjoins it as an indispensable duty. Nothing undoubtedly is more conformable to humanity, than to succour the unfortunate, to clothe the naked, to extend the hand of beneficence to every one in distress. But would it not be more humane and charitable to prevent the source of misery and poverty? If Religion, instead of deifying princes, had taught them to respect the property of their subjects, to be just, to exercise only their lawful rights, we should not be shocked by the sight of such a multitude of beggars. A rapacious, unjust, tyrannical government multiplies misery; heavy taxes produce discouragement, sloth, and poverty, which in their turn beget robberies, assassinations, and crimes of every description. Had sovereigns more humanity, charity, and equity, their dominions would not be peopled by so many wretches, whose misery it becomes impossible to alleviate.

Christian and Mahometan states are full of large hospitals, richly endowed, in which we admire the pious charity of the kings and sultans, who erected them. But would it not have been more humane to govern the people justly, to render them happy, to excite and favour industry and commerce, and to let men enjoy in safety the fruit of their labours, than to crush them under a despotic yoke, to impoverish them by foolish wars, to reduce them to beggary, in order that luxury may be satisfied, and then to erect splendid buildings, which can contain but a very small portion of those, who have been rendered miserable? Religion has only deluded men; instead of preventing evils, it always applies ineffectual remedies.

The ministers of heaven have always known how to profit by the calamities of others. Public misery is their element. They have every where become administrators of the property of the poor, distributors of alms, depositaries of charitable donations; and thereby they have at all times extended and supported their power over the unhappy, who generally compose the most numerous, restless, and seditious part of society. Thus the greatest evils turn to the profit of the ministers of the Lord. Christian priests tell us, that the property they possess is the property of the poor, and that it is therefore sacred. Consequently they have eagerly accumulated lands, revenues, and treasures. Under colour of charity, spiritual guides have become extremely opulent, and in the face of impoverished nations enjoy wealth, which was destined solely for the unfortunate; while the latter, far from murmuring, applaud a pious generosity, which enriches the church, but rarely contributes to the relief of the poor.

According to the principles of Christianity, poverty itself is a virtue; indeed, it is the virtue, which sovereigns and priests oblige their slaves to observe most rigorously. With this idea, many pious Christians have of their own accord renounced riches, distributed their patrimony among the poor, and retired into deserts, there to live in voluntary indigence. But this enthusiasm, this supernatural taste for misery, has been soon forced to yield to nature. The successors of these volunteers in poverty sold to the devout people their prayers, and their intercessions with the Deity. They became rich and powerful. Thus monks and hermits lived in indolence, and under colour of charity, impudently devoured the substance of the poor.

The species of poverty, most esteemed by Religion, is *poverty of mind*. The fundamental virtue of every Religion, most useful to its ministers, is *faith*. It consists in unbounded credulity, which admits, without enquiry, whatever the interpreters of the Deity are interested in making men believe. By the aid of this wonderful virtue, priests became the arbiters of right and wrong, of good and evil: they could easily cause the commission of crimes to advance their interest. Implicit faith has been the source of the greatest outrages that have been committed.

170. He, who first taught nations, that, when we wrong Man, we must ask pardon of God, appease *him* by presents, and offer *him* sacrifices, evidently destroyed the true principles of Morality. According to such ideas, many persons imagine that they may obtain of the king of heaven, as of kings of the earth, permission to be unjust and wicked, or may at least obtain pardon for the evil they may commit.

Morality is founded upon the relations, wants, and constant interests of mankind; the relations, which subsist between God and Men, are either perfectly unknown, or imaginary. Religion, by associating God with Man, has wisely weakened, or destroyed, the bonds, which unite them. Mortals imagine, they may injure one another with impunity, by making suitable satisfaction to the almighty being, who is supposed to have the right of remitting all offences committed against his creatures.

Is any thing better calculated to encourage the wicked or harden them in crimes, than to persuade them that there exists an invisible being, who has a right to forgive acts of injustice, rapine, and outrage committed against society? By these destructive ideas, perverse men perpetrate the most horrid crimes, and believe they make reparation by imploring divine mercy; their conscience is at rest, when a priest assures them that heaven is disarmed by a repentance, which, though sincere, is very useless to the world.

In the mind of a devout man, God must be regarded more than his creatures; it is better to obey him, than men. The interests of the celestial monarch must prevail over those of weak mortals. But the interests of heaven are obviously those of its ministers; whence it evidently follows, that in every religion, priests, under pretext of the interests of heaven or the glory of God, can dispense with the duties of human Morality, when they clash with the duties, which God has a right to impose. Besides, must not he, who has power to pardon crimes, have a right to encourage the commission of crimes?

171. We are perpetually told, that, without a God there would be no *moral obligation*; that the people and even the sovereigns require a legislator powerful enough to constrain them. Moral constraint supposes a law; but this law arises from the eternal and necessary relations of things with one another; relations, which have nothing common with the existence of a God. The rules of Man's conduct are derived from his own nature which he is capable of knowing, and not from the Divine nature of which he has no idea. These rules constrain or oblige us; that is, we render ourselves estimable or contemptible, amiable or detestable, worthy of reward or of punishment, happy or unhappy, accordingly as we conform to, or deviate from these rules. The law, which obliges man not to hurt himself, is founded upon the nature of a sensible being, who, in whatever way he came into this world, is forced by his actual essence to seek good and shun evil, to love pleasure and fear pain. The law, which obliges man not to injure, and even to do good to others, is founded upon the nature of sensible beings, living in society, whose essence compels them to despise those who are useless, and to detest those who oppose their felicity.

Whether there exists a God or not, whether this God has spoken or not, the moral duties of men will be always the same, so long as they are sensible beings. Have men then need of a God whom they know not, of an invisible legislator, of a mysterious religion and of chimerical fears, in order to learn that every excess evidently tends to destroy them, that to preserve health they must be temperate; that to gain the love of others it is necessary to do them good, that to do them evil is a sure means to incur their vengeance and hatred? "Before the law there was no sin." Nothing is more false than this maxim. It suffices that man is what he is, or that he is a sensible being, in order to distinguish what gives him pleasure or displeasure. It suffices that one man knows that another man is a sensible being like himself, to perceive what is useful or hurtful to him. It suffices that man needs his fellow-creature, in order to know that he must fear to excite sentiments unfavourable to himself. Thus the feeling and thinking being has only to feel and think, in order to discover what he must do for himself and others. I feel, and another feels like me; this is the foundation of all morals.

172. We can judge of the goodness of a system of Morals, only by its conformity to the nature of man. By this comparison, we have a right to reject it, if contrary to the welfare of our species. Whoever has seriously meditated Religion; whoever has carefully weighed its advantages and disadvantages, will be fully convinced, that both are injurious to the interests of Man, or directly opposite to his nature.

"To arms! the cause of your God is at stake! Heaven is outraged! The faith is in danger! Impiety! blasphemy! heresy!" The magical power of these formidable words, the real value of which the people never understand, have at all times enabled priests to excite revolts, to dethrone kings, to kindle civil wars, and to lay waste. If we examine the important objects, which have produced so many ravages upon earth, it appears, that either the foolish reveries and whimsical conjectures of some theologian who did not understand himself, or else the pretensions of the clergy, have broken every social bond and deluged mankind with blood and tears.

173. The sovereigns of this world, by associating the Divinity in the government of their dominions, by proclaiming themselves his vicegerents and representatives upon earth, and by acknowledging they hold their power from him, have necessarily constituted his ministers their own rivals or masters. Is it then astonishing, that priests have often made kings feel the superiority of the Celestial Monarch? Have they not more than once convinced temporal princes, that even the greatest power is compelled to yield to the spiritual power of opinion? Nothing is more difficult than to serve two masters, especially when they are not agreed upon what they require.

The association of Religion with Politics necessarily introduced double legislation. The law of God, interpreted by his priests, was often repugnant to the law of the sovereign, or the interest of the state. When princes have firmness and are confident of the love of their subjects, the law of God is sometimes forced to yield to the wise intentions of the temporal sovereign; but generally the *sovereign* authority is obliged to give way to the *divine* authority, that is, to the interests of the clergy. Nothing is more dangerous to a prince, than to *encroach upon the authority of the Church*, that is, to attempt to reform abuses consecrated by religion. God is never more angry than when we touch the divine rights, privileges, possessions, or immunities of his priests.

The metaphysical speculations or religious opinions of men influence their conduct, only when they judge them conformable to their interest. Nothing proves this truth more clearly, than the conduct of many princes with respect to the spiritual power, which they often resist. Ought not a sovereign, persuaded of the importance and rights of Religion, to believe himself in conscience bound to receive respectfully the orders of its priests, and to regard them as the orders of the Divinity? There was a time, when kings and people, more consistent in their conduct, were convinced of the rights of spiritual power, and becoming its slaves, yielded to it upon every occasion, and were but docile instruments in its hands. That happy time is passed. By a strange inconsistency the most devout monarchs are sometimes seen to oppose the enterprises of those, whom they yet regard as the ministers of God. A sovereign, deeply religious, ought to remain prostrate at the feet of his ministers, and regard them as true sovereigns. Is there upon earth a power which has a right to put itself in competition with that of the Most High?

174. Have princes then, who imagine themselves interested in cherishing the prejudices of their subjects, seriously reflected upon the effects, which have been, and may be again produced by certain privileged demagogues, who have a right to speak at pleasure, and in the name of heaven to inflame the passions of millions of subjects? What ravages would not these sacred haranguers cause, if they should conspire, as they have so often done, to disturb the tranquillity of a state!

To most nations, nothing is more burthensome and ruinous than the worship of their gods. Not only do the ministers of these gods every where constitute the first order in the state, but they also enjoy the largest portion of the goods of society, and have a right to levy permanent taxes upon their fellow-citizens. What real advantages then do these organs of the Most High procure the people, for the immense profits extorted from their industry? In exchange for their riches and benefits, what do they give them but mysteries, hypotheses, ceremonies, subtle questions, and endless quarrels, which states are again compelled to pay with blood?

175. Religion, though said to be the firmest prop of Morality, evidently destroys its true springs, in order to substitute imaginary ones, inconceivable chimeras, which, being obviously contrary to reason, nobody firmly believes. All nations declare that they firmly believe in a God, who rewards and punishes; all say they are persuaded of the existence of hell and paradise; yet, do these ideas render men better or counteract the most trifling interests? Every one assures us, that he trembles at the judgments of God; yet every one follows his passions, when he thinks himself sure of escaping the judgments of Man. The fear of invisible powers is seldom so strong as the fear of visible ones. Unknown or remote punishments strike the multitude far less forcibly than the sight of the gallows. Few courtiers fear the anger of their God so much as the displeasure of their master. A pension, a title, or a riband suffices to efface the remembrance both of the torments of hell, and of the pleasures of the celestial court. The caresses of a woman repeatedly prevail over the menaces of the Most High. A jest, a stroke of ridicule, a witticism, make more impression upon the man of the world, than all the grave notions of his Religion.

Are we not assured that *a true repentance* is enough to appease the Deity? Yet we do not see that this *true repentance* is very sincere; at least, it is rare to see noted thieves, even at the point of death, restore goods, which they have unjustly acquired. Men are undoubtedly persuaded, that they shall fit themselves for eternal fire, if they cannot insure themselves against it. But, "Some useful compacts may be made with heaven." By giving the church a part of his fortune, almost every devout rogue may die in peace, without concerning himself in what he gained his riches.

176. By the confession of the warmest defenders of Religion and of its utility, nothing is more rare than sincere conversions, and, we might add, nothing more unprofitable to society. Men are not disgusted with the world, until the world is disgusted with them.

If the devout have the talent of pleasing God and his priests, they have seldom that of being agreeable or useful to society. To a devotee, Religion is a veil, which covers all passions; pride, ill-humour, anger, revenge, impatience, and rancour. Devotion arrogates a tyrannical superiority, which banishes gentleness, indulgence, and gaiety; it authorizes people to censure their neighbours, to reprove and revile the profane for the greater glory of God. It is very common to be devout, and at the same time destitute of every virtue and quality necessary to social life.

177. It is asserted, that the dogma of another life is of the utmost importance to peace and happiness; that without it, men would be destitute of motives to do good. What need is there of terrors and fables to make man sensible how he ought to conduct himself? Does not every one see, that he has the greatest interest, in meriting the approbation, esteem, and benevolence of the beings who surround him, and in abstaining from every thing, by which he may incur the censure, contempt, and resentment of society? However short an entertainment, a conversation, or visit, does not each desire to act his part decently, and agreeably to himself and others? If life is but a passage, let us strive to make it easy; which we cannot effect, if we fail in regard for those who travel with us. Religion, occupied with its gloomy reveries, considers man merely as a pilgrim upon earth; and therefore supposes that, in order to travel the more securely, he must forsake company, and deprive himself of pleasure and amusements, which might console him for the tediousness and fatigue of the journey. A stoical and morose philosopher sometimes gives us advice as irrational as that of Religion. But a more rational philosophy invites us to spread flowers upon the way of life, to dispel melancholy and banish terrors, to connect our interest with that of our fellow-travellers, and by gaiety and lawful pleasures, to divert our attention from difficulties and accidents, to which we are often exposed; it teaches us, that, to travel agreeably, we should abstain from what might be injurious to ourselves, and carefully shun what might render us odious to our associates.

178. It is asked, *what motives an Atheist can have to do good?* The motive to please himself and his fellow-creatures; to live happily and peaceably; to gain the affection and esteem of men. "Can he, who fears not the gods, fear any thing?" He can fear men; he can fear contempt, dishonour, the punishment of the laws; in short, he can fear himself, and the remorse felt by all those who are conscious of having incurred or merited the hatred of their fellow-creatures.

Conscience is the internal testimony, which we bear to ourselves, of having acted so as to merit the esteem or blame of the beings, with whom we live; and it is founded upon the clear knowledge we have of men, and of the sentiments which our actions must produce in them. The Conscience of the religious man consists in imagining that he has pleased or displeased his God, of whom he has no idea, and whose obscure and doubtful intentions are explained to him only by men of doubtful veracity, who, like him, are utterly unacquainted with the essence of the Deity, and are little agreed upon what can please or displease him. In a word, the conscience of the credulous is directed by men, who have themselves an erroneous conscience, or whose interest stifles knowledge.

"Can an Atheist have a Conscience? What are his motives to abstain from hidden vices and secret crimes of which other men are ignorant, and which are beyond the reach of laws?" He may be assured by constant experience, that there is no vice, which, by the nature of things, does not punish itself. Would he preserve this life? he will avoid every excess, that may impair his health; he will not wish to lead a languishing life, which would render him a burden to himself and others. As for secret crimes, he will abstain from them, for fear he shall be forced to blush at himself, from whom he cannot flee. If he has any reason, he will know the value of the esteem which an honest man ought to have for himself. He will see, that unforeseen circumstances may unveil the conduct, which he feels interested in concealing from others. The other world furnishes no motives for doing good, to him, who finds none on earth.

179. "The speculative Atheist," says the Theist, "may be an honest man, but his writings will make political Atheists. Princes and ministers, no longer restrained by the fear of God, will abandon themselves, without scruple, to the most horrid excesses." But, however great the depravity of an Atheist upon the throne, can it be stronger and more destructive, than that of the many conquerors, tyrants, persecutors, ambitious men, and perverse courtiers, who, though not Atheists, but often very religious and devout, have notwithstanding made humanity groan under the weight of their crimes? Can an atheistical prince do more harm to the world, than a Louis XI., a Philip II., a Richelieu, who all united Religion with crime? Nothing is more rare, than atheistical princes; nothing more common, than tyrants and ministers, who are very wicked and very religious.

180. A man of reflection cannot be incapable of his duties, of discovering the relations subsisting between men, of meditating his own nature, of discerning his

own wants, propensities, and desires, and of perceiving what he owes to beings, who are necessary to his happiness. These reflections naturally lead him to a knowledge of the Morality most essential to social beings. Dangerous passions seldom fall to the lot of a man who loves to commune with himself, to study, and to investigate the principles of things. The strongest passion of such a man will be to know truth, and his ambition to teach it to others. Philosophy cultivates the mind. On the score of morals and honesty, has not he who reflects and reasons, evidently an advantage over him, who makes it a principle never to reason?

If ignorance is useful to priests, and to the oppressors of mankind, it is fatal to society. Man, void of knowledge, does not enjoy reason; without reason and knowledge, he is a savage, liable to commit crimes. Morality, or the science of duties, is acquired only by the study of Man, and of what is relative to Man. He, who does not reflect, is unacquainted with true Morality, and walks with precarious steps, in the path of virtue. The less men reason, the more wicked they are. Savages, princes, nobles, and the dregs of the people, are commonly the worst of men, because they reason the least. The devout man seldom reflects, and rarely reasons. He fears all enquiry, scrupulously follows authority, and often, through an error of conscience, makes it a sacred duty to commit evil. The Atheist reasons: he consults experience, which he prefers to prejudice. If he reasons justly, his conscience is enlightened; he finds more real motives to do good than the bigot whose only motives are his fallacies, and who never listens to reason. Are not the motives of the Atheist sufficiently powerful to counteract his passions? Is he blind enough to be unmindful of his true interest, which ought to restrain him? But he will be neither worse nor better, than the numerous believers, who, notwithstanding Religion and its sublime precepts, follow a conduct which Religion condemns. Is a credulous assassin less to be feared, than an assassin who believes nothing? Is a very devout tyrant less tyrannical than an undevout tyrant?

181. Nothing is more uncommon, than to see men consistent. Their opinions never influence their conduct except when conformable to their temperaments, passions, and interests. Daily experience shows, that religious opinions produce much evil and little good. They are hurtful, because they often favour the passions of tyrants, of ambitious men, of fanatics, and of priests; they are of no effect, because incapable of counter-balancing the present interests of the greater part of mankind.

Religious principles are of no avail, when they act in opposition to ardent desires; though not unbelievers, men then conduct themselves as if they believed nothing.

We shall always be liable to err, when we judge of the opinions of men by their conduct, or of their conduct by their opinions. A religious man, notwithstanding the unsociable principles of a sanguinary religion, will sometimes by a happy inconsistency, be humane, tolerant, and moderate; the principles of his religion do not then agree with the gentleness of his character. Libertines, debauchees, hypocrites, adulterers, and rogues, often appear to have the best ideas upon morals. Why do they not reduce them to practice? Because their temperament, their interest, and their habits do not accord with their sublime theories. The rigid principles of Christian morality, which many people regard as divine, have but little influence upon the conduct of those, who preach them to others. Do they not daily tell us, *to do what they preach, and not what they practise?*

The partisans of Religion often denote an infidel by the word *libertine*. It is possible that many unbelievers may have loose morals, which is owing to their temperament, and not to their opinions. But how does their conduct affect their opinions? Cannot then an immoral man be a good physician, architect, geometrician, logician, or metaphysician? A man of irreproachable conduct may be extremely deficient in knowledge and reason. In quest of truth, it little concerns us from whom it comes. Let us not judge men by their opinions, nor opinions by men; let us judge men by their conduct, and their opinions by their conformity with experience and reason and by their utility to mankind.

182. Every man, who reasons, soon becomes an unbeliever; for reason shows, that theology is nothing but a tissue of chimeras; that religion is contrary to every principle of good sense, that it tinctures all human knowledge with falsity. The sensible man is an unbeliever, because he sees, that, far from making men happier, religion is the chief source of the greatest disorders, and the permanent calamities, with which man is afflicted. The man, who seeks his own welfare and tranquillity, examines and throws aside religion, because he thinks it no less troublesome than useless, to spend his life in trembling before phantoms, fit to impose only upon silly women or children.

If licentiousness, which reasons but little, sometimes leads to irreligion, the man of pure morals may have very good motives for examining his religion, and banishing it from his mind. Religious terrors, too weak to impose upon the wicked in whom vice is deeply rooted, afflict, torment and overwhelm restless imaginations. Courageous and vigorous minds soon shake off the insupportable yoke. But those, who are weak and timorous, languish under it during life; and as they grow old their fears increase.

Priests have represented God as so malicious, austere, and terrible a being, that most men would cordially wish, that there was no God. It is impossible to be happy, while always trembling. Ye devout! you adore a terrible God! But you hate him; you would be glad, if he did not exist. Can we refrain from desiring the absence or destruction of a master, the idea of whom destroys our happiness? The black colours, in which priests paint the Divinity, are truly shocking, and force us to hate and reject him.

183. If fear created the gods, fear supports their empire over the minds of mortals. So early are men accustomed to shudder at the mere name of the Deity, that they regard him as a spectre, a hobgoblin, a bugbear, which torments and deprives them of courage even to wish relief from their fears. They apprehend, that the invisible spectre, will strike them the moment they cease to be afraid. Bigots are too much in fear of their God to love him sincerely. They serve him like slaves, who, unable to escape his power, resolve to flatter their master, and who, by dint of lying, at length persuade themselves, that they in some measure love him. They make a virtue of necessity. The love of devotees for their God, and of slaves for their despots, is only a feigned homage.

184. Christian divines have represented their God so terrible and so little worthy of love, that several of them have thought they must dispense with loving him; a blasphemy, shocking to other divines, who were less ingenuous. St. Thomas having maintained, that we are obliged to love God as soon as we attain the use of reason, the Jesuit Sirmond answered him, *that is very soon*. The Jesuit Vasquez assures us, that *it is enough to love God at the point of death*. Hurtado, more rigid, says, *we must love God very year*. Henriquez is contented that we love him *every five years*; Sotus, *every Sunday*. Upon what are these opinions grounded? asks father Sirmond; who adds, that Suarez requires us to *love God sometimes*. But when? He leaves that to us; he knows nothing about it himself. *Now*, says he, *who will be able to know that, of which such a learned divine is ignorant?* The same Jesuit Sirmond further observes, that *God*

"does not command us to love him with an affectionate love, nor does he promise us salvation upon condition that we give him our hearts; it is enough to obey and love him with an effective love by executing his orders; this is the only love we owe him; and he has not so much commanded us to love him, as not to hate him." This doctrine appears heretical, impious, and abominable to the Jansenists, who, by the revolting severity they attribute to their God, make him far less amiable, than the Jesuits, their adversaries. The latter, to gain adherents, paint God in colours capable of encouraging the most perverse of mortals. Thus nothing is more undecided with the Christians, than the important question, whether they can, ought, or ought not to love God. Some of their spiritual guides maintain, that it is necessary to love him with all one's heart, notwithstanding all his severity; others, like father Daniel, think that, *an act of pure love to God is the most heroic act of Christian virtue, and almost beyond the reach of human weakness*. The Jesuit Pintereau goes farther; he says, *a deliverance from the grievous yoke of loving God is a privilege of the new covenant*.

185. The character of the Man always decides that of his God; every body makes one for himself and like himself. The man of gaiety, involved in dissipation and pleasure, does not imagine, that, God can be stern and cross; he wants a good-natured God, with whom he can find reconciliation. The man of a rigid, morose, bilious, sour disposition, must have a God like himself, a God of terror; and he regards, as perverse, those, who admit a placable, indulgent God. As men are constituted, organized, and modified in a manner, which cannot be precisely the same, how can they agree about a chimera, which exists only in their brains?

The cruel and endless disputes between the ministers of the Lord, are not such as to attract the confidence of those, who impartially consider them. How can we avoid complete infidelity, upon viewing principles, about which those who teach them to others are never agreed? How can we help doubting the existence of a God, of whom it is evident that even his ministers can only form very fluctuating ideas? How can we in short avoid totally rejecting a God, who is nothing but a shapeless heap of contradictions? How can we refer the matter to the decision of priests, who are perpetually at war, treating each other as impious and heretical, defaming and persecuting each other without mercy, for differing in the manner of understanding what they announce to the world?

186. The existence of a God is the basis of all Religion. Nevertheless, this im-

portant truth has not as yet been demonstrated, I do not say so as to convince unbelievers, but in a manner satisfactory to theologians themselves. Profound thinkers have at all times been occupied in inventing new proofs. What are the fruits of their meditations and arguments? They have left the subject in a worse condition; they have demonstrated nothing; they have almost always excited the clamours of their brethren, who have accused them of having poorly defended the best of causes.

187. The apologists of religion daily repeat, that the passions alone make unbelievers. "Pride," say they, "and the desire of signalizing themselves, make men Atheists. They endeavour to efface from their minds the idea of God, only because they have reason to fear his terrible judgments." Whatever may be the motives, which incline men to Atheism, it is our business to examine, whether their sentiments are founded in truth. No man acts without motives. Let us first examine the arguments and afterwards the motives. We shall see whether these motives are not legitimate, and more rational than those of many credulous bigots, who suffer themselves to be guided by masters little worthy of the confidence of men.

You say then, Priests of the Lord! that the passions make unbelievers; that they renounce Religion only through interest, or because it contradicts their inordinate propensities; you assert, that they attack your gods only because they fear their severity. But, are you yourselves, in defending Religion and its chimeras, truly exempt from passions and interests? Who reap advantages from this Religion, for which priests display so much zeal? Priests. To whom does Religion procure power, influence, riches, and honours? To Priests. Who wage war, in every country, against reason, science, truth, and philosophy, and render them odious to sovereigns and people? Priests. Who profit by the ignorance and vain prejudices of men? Priests.-- Priests! you are rewarded, honoured and paid for deceiving mortals, and you cause those to be punished who undeceive them. The follies of men procure you benefices, offerings, and expiations; while those, who announce the most useful truths, are rewarded only with chains, gibbets and funeral-piles. Let the world judge between us.

188. Pride and vanity have been, and ever will be, inherent in the priesthood. Is any thing more capable of rendering men haughty and vain, than the pretence of exercising a power derived from heaven, of bearing a sacred character, of being the messengers and ministers of the Most High? Are not these dispositions perpetually

nourished by the credulity of the people, the deference and respect of sovereigns, the immunities, privileges, and distinctions enjoyed by the clergy? In every country, the vulgar are much more devoted to their spiritual guides, whom they regard as divine, than to their temporal superiors, whom they consider as no more than ordinary men. The parson of a village acts a much more conspicuous part, than the lord of the manor or the justice of the peace. Among the Christians, a priest thinks himself far above a king or an emperor. A Spanish grandee having spoken rather haughtily to a monk, the latter arrogantly said, "Learn to respect a man, who daily has your God in his hands, and your Queen at his feet." Have priests then a right to accuse unbelievers of pride? Are they themselves remarkable for uncommon modesty or profound humility? Is it not evident, that the desire of domineering over men is essential to their trade? If the ministers of the Lord were truly modest, should we see them so greedy of respect, so impatient of contradiction, so positive in their decisions, and so unmercifully revengeful to those whose opinions offend them? Has not Science the modesty to acknowledge how difficult it is to discover truth? What other passion but ungovernable pride can make men so savage, revengeful, and void of indulgence and gentleness? What can be more presumptuous, than to arm nations and deluge the world in blood, in order to establish or defend futile conjectures?

You say, that presumption alone makes Atheists. Inform them then what your God is; teach them his essence; speak of him intelligibly; say something about him, which is reasonable, and not contradictory or impossible. If you are unable to satisfy them, if hitherto none of you have been able to demonstrate the existence of a God in a clear and convincing manner; if by your own confession, his essence is completely veiled from you, as from the rest of mortals, forgive those, who cannot admit what they can neither understand nor make consistent with itself; do not tax with presumption and vanity those who are sincere enough to confess their ignorance; do not accuse of folly those who find themselves incapable of believing contradictions; and for once, blush at exciting the hatred and fury of sovereigns and people against men, who think not like you concerning a being, of whom you have no idea. Is any thing more rash and extravagant, than to reason concerning an object, known to be inconceivable? You say, that the corruption of the heart produces Atheism, that men shake off the yoke of the Deity only because they fear his formidable judgments. But, why do you paint your God in colours so shocking, that he becomes insupportable? Why does so powerful a God permit men to be so corrupt? How can we help endeavouring to shake off the yoke of a tyrant, who, able to do as he pleases with men, consents to their perversion, who hardens, and blinds them, and refuses them his grace, that he may have the satisfaction to punish them eternally, for having been hardened, and blinded, and for not having the grace which he refused? Theologians and priests must be very confident of the grace of heaven and a happy futurity, to refrain from detesting a master so capricious as the God they announce. A God, who damns eternally, is the most odious of beings that the human mind can invent.

189. No man upon earth is truly interested in the support of error, which is forced sooner or later to yield to truth. The general good must at length open the eyes of mortals: the passions themselves sometimes contribute to break the chains of prejudices. Did not the passions of sovereigns, centuries ago, annihilate in some countries of Europe the tyrannical power, which a too haughty pontiff once exercised over all princes of his sect? In consequence of the progress of political science, the clergy were then stripped of immense riches, which credulity had accumulated upon them. Ought not this memorable example to convince priests, that prejudices triumph but for a time, and that truth alone can insure solid happiness?

By caressing sovereigns, by fabricating divine rights for them, by deifying them, and by abandoning the people, bound hand and foot, to their will, the ministers of the Most High must see, that they are labouring to make them tyrants. Have they not reason to apprehend, that the gigantic idols, which they raised to the clouds, will one day crush them by their enormous weight? Do not a thousand examples remind them that these tyrants, after preying upon the people, may prey upon them in their turn.

We will respect priests, when they become sensible men. Let them, if they please, use the authority of heaven to frighten those princes who are continually desolating the earth; but let them no more adjudge to them the horrid right of being unjust with impunity. Let them acknowledge, that no man is interested in living under tyranny; and let them teach sovereigns, that they themselves are not interested in exercising a despotism, which, by rendering them odious, exposes them to danger, and detracts from their power and greatness. Finally, let priests and kings become so far enlightened as to acknowledge, that no power is secure which is not founded upon truth, reason, and equity.

190. By waging war against Reason, which they ought to have protected and developed, the ministers of the gods evidently act against their own interest. What power, influence, and respect might they not have gained among the wisest of men, what gratitude would they not have excited in the people, if, instead of wasting their time about their vain disputes, they had applied themselves to really useful science, and investigated the true principles of philosophy, government, and morals! Who would dare to reproach a body with its opulence or influence, if the members dedicating themselves to the public good, employed their leisure in study, and exercised their authority in enlightening the minds both of sovereigns and subjects?

Priests! Forsake your chimeras, your unintelligible dogmas, your contemptible quarrels! Banish those phantoms which could be useful only in the infancy of nations. Assume, at length, the language of reason. Instead of exciting persecution; instead of entertaining the people with silly disputes; instead of preaching useless and fanatical dogmas, preach human and social morality; preach virtues really useful to the world; become the apostles of reason, the defenders of liberty, and the reformers of abuses.

191. Philosophers have every where taken upon themselves a part, which seemed destined to the ministers of Religion. The hatred of the latter for philosophy was only a jealousy of trade. But, instead of endeavouring to injure and decry each other, all men of good sense should unite their efforts to combat error, seek truth, and especially to put to flight the prejudices, that are equally injurious to sovereigns and subjects, and of which the abettors themselves sooner or later become the victims.

In the hands of an enlightened government, the priests would become the most useful of the citizens. Already richly paid by the state, and free from the care of providing for their own subsistence, how could they be better employed than in qualifying themselves for the instruction of others? Would not their minds be better satisfied with discovering luminous truths, than in wandering through the thick darkness of error? Would it be more difficult to discern the clear principles of Morality, than the imaginary principles of a divine and theological Morality? Would men of ordinary capacities find it as difficult to fix in their heads the simple notions of their duties, as to load their memories with mysteries, unintelligible words and obscure definitions, of which they can never form a clear idea? What time and pains are lost in learning and teaching things, which are not of the least real utility! What resources for the encouragement of the sciences, the advancement of knowledge, and the education of youth, well disposed sovereigns might find in the many monasteries, which in several countries live upon the people without in the slightest degree profiting them! But superstition, jealous of its exclusive empire, seems resolved to form only useless beings. To what advantage might we not turn a multitude of cenobites of both sexes, who, in many countries, are amply endowed for doing nothing? Instead of overwhelming them with fasting and austerities; instead of barren contemplations, mechanical prayers, and trifling ceremonies; why should we not excite in them a salutary emulation, which may incline them to seek the means, not of being *dead* to the world, but of being *useful* to it? Instead of filling the youthful minds of their pupils with fables, sterile dogmas, and puerilities, why are not priests obliged, or invited to teach them truths, and to render them useful citizens of their country? Under the present system, men are only useful to the clergy who blind them, and to the tyrants who fleece them.

192. The partisans of credulity often accuse unbelievers of insincerity, because they sometimes waver in their principles, alter their minds in sickness, and retract at death. When the body is disordered, the faculty of reasoning is commonly disordered with it. At the approach of death, man, weak and decayed, is sometimes himself sensible that Reason abandons him, and that Prejudice returns. There are some diseases, which tend to weaken the brain; to create despondency and pusillanimity; and there are others, which destroy the body, but do not disturb the reason. At any rate, an unbeliever who recants in sickness is not more extraordinary, than a devotee who neglects in health the duties which his religion explicitly enjoins.

Ministers of Religion openly contradict in their daily conduct the rigorous principles, they teach to others; in consequence of which, unbelievers, in their turn, may justly accuse them of insincerity. Is it easy to find many prelates humble, generous, void of ambition, enemies of pomp and grandeur, and friends of poverty? In short, is the conduct of Christian ministers conformable to the austere morality of Christ, their God, and their model?

193. *Atheism*, it is said, *breaks all the ties of society. Without the belief of a God, what*

will become of the sacredness of oaths? How shall we oblige a man to speak the, truth, who cannot seriously call the Deity to witness what he says? But, does an oath strengthen our obligation to fulfil the engagements contracted? Will he, who is not fearful of lying, be less fearful of perjury? He, who is base enough to break his word, or unjust enough to violate his engagements, in contempt of the esteem of men, will not be more faithful therein for having called all the gods to witness his oaths. Those, who disregard the judgments of men, will soon disregard the judgments of God. Are not princes, of all men, the most ready to swear, and the most ready to violate their oaths?

194. *The vulgar*, it is repeatedly said, *must have a Religion. If enlightened persons have no need of the restraint of opinion, it is at least necessary to rude men, whose reason is uncultivated by education*. But, is it indeed a fact, that religion is a restraint upon the vulgar? Do we see, that this religion preserves them from intemperance, drunkenness, brutality, violence, fraud, and every kind of excess? Could a people who have no idea of the Deity conduct themselves in a more detestable manner, than these believing people, among whom we find dissipation and vices, the most unworthy of reasonable beings? Upon going out of the churches, do not the working classes, and the populace, plunge without fear into their ordinary irregularities, under the idea, that the periodical homage, which they render to their God, authorizes them to follow, without remorse, their vicious habits and pernicious propensities? Finally, if the people are so low-minded and unreasonable, is not their stupidity chargeable to the negligence of their princes, who are wholly regardless of public education, or who even oppose the instruction of their subjects? Is not the want of reason in the people evidently the work of the priests, who, instead of instructing men in a rational morality, entertain them with fables, reveries, ceremonies, fallacies, and false virtues which they think of the greatest importance?

To the people, Religion is but a vain display of ceremonies, to which they are attached by habit, which entertains their eyes, and produces a transient emotion in their torpid understandings, without influencing their conduct or reforming their morals. Even by the confession of the ministers of the altars, nothing is more rare than that *internal* and *spiritual* Religion, which alone is capable of regulating the life of man and of triumphing over his evil propensities. In the most numerous and devout nation, are there many persons, who are really capable of understanding the principles of their religious system, and who find them powerful enough to stifle their perverse inclinations?

Many persons will say, that *any restraint whatever is better than none*. They will maintain, that *if religion awes not the greater part, it serves at least to restrain some individuals, who would otherwise without remorse abandon themselves to crime*. Men ought undoubtedly to have a restraint, but not an imaginary one. Religion only frightens those whose imbecility of character has already prevented them from being formidable to their fellow-citizens. An equitable government, severe laws, and sound morality have an equal power over all; at least, every person must believe in them, and perceive the danger of not conforming to them.

195. Perhaps it will be asked, *whether Atheism can be proper for the multitude?* I answer, that any system, which requires discussion, is not made for the multitude. *What purpose then can it serve to preach Atheism?* It may at least serve to convince all those who reason, that nothing is more extravagant than to fret one's self, and nothing more unjust than to vex others, for mere groundless conjectures. As for the vulgar who never reason, the arguments of an Atheist are no more fit for them than the systems of a natural philosopher, the observations of an astronomer, the experiments of a chemist, the calculations of a geometrician, the researches of a physician, the plans of an architect, or the pleadings of a lawyer, who all labour for the people without their knowledge.

Are the metaphysical reasonings and religious disputes, which have so long engrossed the time and attention of so many profound thinkers, better adapted to the generality of men than the reasoning of an Atheist? Nay, as the principles of Atheism are founded upon plain common sense, are they not more intelligible, than those of a theology, beset with difficulties, which even the persons of the greatest genius cannot explain? In every country, the people have a religion, the principles of which they are totally ignorant, and which they follow from habit without any examination: their priests alone are engaged in theology, which is too dense for vulgar heads. If the people should chance to lose this unknown theology, they mighty easily console themselves for the loss of a thing, not only perfectly useless, but also productive of dangerous commotions.

It would be madness to write for the vulgar, or to attempt to cure their prejudices all at once. We write for those only, who read and reason; the multitude read but little, and reason still less. Calm and rational persons will require new ideas, and knowledge will be gradually diffused.

196. If theology is a branch of commerce profitable to theologians, it is evidently not only superfluous, but injurious to the rest of society. Self-interest will sooner or later open the eyes of men. Sovereigns and subjects will one day adopt the profound indifference and contempt, merited by a futile system, which serves only to make men miserable. All persons will be sensible of the inutility of the many expensive ceremonies, which contribute nothing to public felicity. Contemptible quarrels will cease to disturb the tranquility of states, when we blush at having considered them important.

Instead of Parliament meddling with the senseless combats of your clergy; instead of foolishly espousing their impertinent quarrels, and attempting to make your subjects adopt uniform opinions--strive to make them happy in this world. Respect their liberty and property, watch over their education, encourage them in their labours, reward their talents and virtues, repress licentiousness; and do not concern yourselves with their manner of thinking. Theological fables are useful only to tyrants and the ignorant.

197. Does it then require an extraordinary effort of genius to comprehend, that what is above the capacity of man, is not made for him; that things supernatural are not made for natural beings; that impenetrable mysteries are not made for limited minds? If theologians are foolish enough to dispute upon objects, which they acknowledge to be unintelligible even to themselves, ought society to take any part in their silly quarrels? Must the blood of nations flow to enhance the conjectures of a few infatuated dreamers? If it is difficult to cure theologians of their madness and the people of their prejudices, it is at least easy to prevent the extravagancies of one party, and the silliness of the other from producing pernicious effects. Let every one be permitted to think as he pleases; but never let him be permitted to injure others for their manner of thinking. Were the rulers of nations more just and rational, theological opinions would not affect the public tranquillity, more than the disputes of natural philosophers, physicians, grammarians, and critics. It is tyranny which causes theological quarrels to be attended with serious consequences.

Those, who extol the importance and utility of Religion, ought to shew us its happy effects, the advantages for instance, which the disputes and abstract speculations of theology can be to porters, artisans, and labourers, and to the multitude of unfortunate women and corrupt servants with which great cities abound. All these beings are religious; they have what is called *an implicit faith*. Their parsons believe for them; and they stupidly adhere to the unknown belief of their guides. They go to hear sermons, and would think it a great crime to transgress any of the ordinances, to which, in childhood, they are taught to conform. But of what service to morals is all this? None at all. They have not the least idea of Morality, and are even guilty of all the roguery, fraud, rapine, and excess, that is out of the reach of law.

The populace have no idea of their Religion; what they call Religion is nothing but a blind attachment to unknown opinions and mysterious practices. In fact, to deprive people of Religion is to deprive them of nothing. By overthrowing their prejudices, we should only lessen or annihilate the dangerous confidence they put in interested guides, and should teach them to mistrust those, who, under the pretext of Religion, often lead them into fatal excesses.

198. While pretending to instruct and enlighten men, Religion in reality keeps them in ignorance, and stifles the desire of knowing the most interesting objects. The people have no other rule of conduct, than what their priests are pleased to prescribe. Religion supplies the place of every thing else: but being in itself essentially obscure, it is more proper to lead mortals astray than to guide them in the path of science and happiness. Religion renders enigmatical all Natural Philosophy, Morality, Legislation and Politics. A man blinded by religious prejudices, fears truth, whenever it clashes with his opinions: he cannot know his own nature he cannot cultivate his reason, he cannot perform experiments.

Everything concurs to render the people devout; but every thing tends to prevent them from being humane, reasonable and virtuous. Religion seems to have no other object, than to stupefy the mind.

Priests have been ever at war with genius and talent, because well-informed men perceive, that superstition shackles the human mind, and would keep it in eternal infancy, occupied solely by fables and frightened by phantoms. Incapable of improvement itself, Theology opposed insurmountable barriers to the progress of true knowledge; its sole object is to keep nations and their rulers in the most profound ignorance of their duties, and of the real motives, that should incline them to do good. It obscures Morality, renders its principles arbitrary, and subjects it to the caprice of the gods or of their ministers. It converts the art of governing men into a mysterious tyranny, which is the scourge of nations. It changes princes into unjust, licentious despots, and the people into ignorant slaves, who become corrupt in order to merit the favour of their masters.

199. By tracing the history of the human mind, we shall be easily convinced, that Theology has cautiously guarded against its progress. It began by giving out fables as sacred truth: it produced poetry, which filled the imagination of men with its puerile fictions: it entertained them with its gods and their incredible deeds. In a word, Religion has always treated men, like children, whom it lulled to sleep with tales, which its ministers would have us still regard as incontestable truths.

If the ministers of the gods have sometimes made useful discoveries, they have always been careful to give them a dogmatical tone, and envelope them in the shades of mystery. Pythagoras and Plato, in order to acquire some trifling knowledge, were obliged to court the favour of priests, to be initiated in their mysteries, and to undergo whatever trials they were pleased to impose. At this price, they were permitted to imbibe those exalted notions, still so bewitching to all those who admire only what is perfectly unintelligible. It was from Egyptian, Indian, and Chaldean priests, from the schools of these visionaries, professionally interested in bewildering human reason, that philosophy was obliged to borrow its first rudiments. Obscure and false in its principles, mixed with fictions and fables, and made only to dazzle the imagination, the progress of this philosophy was precarious, and its theories unintelligible; instead of enlightening, it blighted the mind, and diverted it from objects truly useful.

The theological speculations and mystical reveries of the ancients are still law in a great part of the philosophic world; and being adopted by modern theology, it is heresy to abandon them. They tell us "of aerial beings, of spirits, angels, demons, genii," and other phantoms, which are the object of their meditations, and serve as the basis of *metaphysics*, an abstract and futile science, which for thousands of years the greatest geniuses have vainly studied. Hypothesis, imagined by a few visionaries of Memphis and Babylon, constitute even now the foundations of a science, whose obscurity makes it revered as marvellous and divine.

The first legislators were priests; the first mythologists, poets, learned men, and physicians were priests. In their hands science became sacred and was withheld from the profane. They spoke only in allegories, emblems, enigmas, and ambiguous oracles--means well calculated to excite curiosity, and above all to inspire the astonished vulgar with a holy respect for men, who when they were thought to be instructed by the gods, and capable of reading in the heavens the fate of the earth, boldly proclaimed themselves the oracles of the Deity.

200. The religions of ancient priests have only changed form. Although our modern theologians regard their predecessors as impostors, yet they have collected many scattered fragments of their religious systems. In modern Religions we find, not only their metaphysical dogmas, which theology has merely clothed in a new dress, but also some remarkable remains of their superstitious practices, their magic, and their enchantments. Christians are still commanded to respect the remaining monuments of the legislators, priests, and prophets of the Hebrew Religion, which had borrowed its strange practices from Egypt. Thus extravagancies, imagined by knaves or idolatrous visionaries, are still sacred among Christians!

If we examine history, we shall find a striking resemblance among all Religions. In all parts of the earth, we see, that religious notions, periodically depress and elevate the people. The attention of man is every where engrossed, by rites often abominable, and by mysteries always formidable, which become the sole objects of meditation. The different superstitions borrow, from one another, their abstract reveries and ceremonies. Religions are in general mere unintelligible rhapsodies, combined by new teachers, who use the materials of their predecessors, reserving the right of adding or retrenching whatever is not conformable to the present age. The religion of Egypt was evidently the basis of the religion of Moses, who banished the worship of idols: Moses was merely a schismatic Egyptian. Christianism is only reformed Judaism. Mahometanism is composed of Judaism, Christianity, and the ancient religion of Arabia, etc.

201. Theology, from the remotest antiquity to the present time, has had the exclusive privilege of directing philosophy. What assistance has been derived from its labours? It changed philosophy into an unintelligible jargon, calculated to render uncertain the clearest truths; it has converted the art of reasoning into a jargon of words; it has carried the human mind into the airy regions of metaphysics, and there employed it in vainly fathoming an obscure abyss. Instead of physical and

simple causes, this transformed philosophy has substituted supernatural, or rather, *occult* causes; it has explained phenomena difficult to be conceived by agents still more inconceivable. It has filled language with words, void of sense, incapable of accounting for things, better calculated to obscure than enlighten, and which seems invented expressly to discourage man, to guard him against the powers of his mind, to make him mistrust the principles of reason and evidence, and to raise an insurmountable barrier between him and truth.

202. Were we to believe the partisans of Religion, nothing could be explained without it; nature would be a perpetual enigma, and man would be incapable of understanding himself. But, what does this Religion in reality explain? The more we examine it, the more we are convinced that its theological notions are fit only to confuse our ideas; they change every thing into mystery: they explain difficult things by things that are impossible. Is it a satisfactory explanation of phenomena, to attribute them to unknown agents, to invisible powers, to immaterial causes? Does the human mind receive much light by being referred to *the depths of the treasures of divine wisdom*, to which, we are repeatedly told, it is vain to extend our rash enquiries? Can the divine nature, of which we have no conception, enable us to conceive the nature of man?

Ask a Christian, what is the origin of the world? He will answer, that God created it. What is God? He cannot tell. What is it to create? He knows not. What is the cause of pestilence, famine, wars, droughts, inundations and earthquakes? The anger of God. What remedies can be applied to these calamities? Prayers, sacrifices, processions, offerings, and ceremonies are, it is said, the true means of disarming celestial fury. But why is heaven enraged? Because men are wicked. Why are men wicked? Because their nature is corrupt. What is the cause of this corruption? It is, says the theologian, because the first man, beguiled by the first woman, ate an apple, which God had forbidden him to touch. Who beguiled this woman into such folly? The devil. Who made the devil? God. But, why did God make this devil, destined to pervert mankind? This is unknown; it is a mystery which the Deity alone is acquainted with.

It is now universally acknowledged, that the earth turns round the sun. Centuries ago, this opinion was blasphemy, as being irreconcileable with the sacred books which every Christian reveres as inspired by the Deity himself. Notwithstanding divine revelation, astronomers now depend rather upon evidence, than upon the testimony of their inspired books.

What is the hidden principle of the motions of the human body? The soul. What is a soul? A spirit. What is a spirit? A substance, which has neither form, nor colour, nor extension, nor parts. How can we form any idea of such a substance? How can it move a body? That is not known; it is a mystery. Have beasts souls? But, do they not act, feel, and think, in a manner very similar to man? Mere illusion! By what right do you deprive beasts of a soul, which you attribute to man, though you know nothing at all about it? Because the souls of beasts would embarrass our theologians, who are satisfied with the power of terrifying and damning the immaterial souls of men, and are not so much interested in damning those of beasts. Such are the puerile solutions, which philosophy, always in the leading strings of theology, was obliged to invent, in order to explain the problems of the physical and moral world?

203. How many evasions have been used, both in ancient and modern times, in order to avoid an engagement with the ministers of the gods, who have ever been the tyrants of thought? How many hypotheses and shifts were such men as Descartes, Mallebranche, and Leibnitz, forced to invent, in order to reconcile their discoveries with the fables and mistakes which Religion had consecrated! In what guarded phrases have the greatest philosophers expressed themselves, even at the risk of being absurd, inconsistent, or unintelligible, whenever their ideas did not accord with the principles of theology! Priests have been always attentive to extinguish systems which opposed their interest. Theology was ever the bed of Procrustes, to be adapted to which, the limbs of travellers, if too long were cut off, and if too short were lengthened.

Can any sensible man, delighted with the sciences and attached to the welfare of his fellow-creatures, reflect, without vexation and anguish, how many profound, laborious, and subtle brains have been for ages foolishly occupied in the study of absurdities? What a treasure of knowledge might have been diffused by many celebrated thinkers, if instead of engaging in the impertinent disputes of vain theology, they had devoted their attention to intelligible objects really important to mankind? Half the efforts which religious opinions have cost genius, and half the wealth which frivolous forms of worship have cost nations would have sufficed to instruct them perfectly in morality, politics, natural philosophy, medicine, agriculture, etc. Superstition generally absorbs the attention, admiration, and treasures of the people; their Religion costs them very dear; but they have neither knowledge, virtue, nor happiness, for their money.

204. Some ancient and modern philosophers have been bold enough to assume experience and reason for their guides, and to shake off the chains of superstition. Democritus, Epicurus, and other Greeks presumed to tear away the veil of prejudice, and to deliver philosophy from theological shackles. But their systems, too simple, too sensible, and too free from the marvellous, for imaginations enamoured with chimeras, were obliged to yield to the fabulous conjectures of such men as Plato and Socrates. Among the moderns, Hobbes, Spinosa, Bayle, etc., have followed the steps of Epicurus; but their doctrine has found very few followers, in a world, still intoxicated with fables, to listen to reason.

In every age, it has been dangerous to depart from prejudices. Discoveries of every kind have been prohibited. All that enlightened men could do, was to speak ambiguously, hence they often confounded falsehood with truth. Several had a *double doctrine*, one public and the other secret; the key of the latter being lost, their true sentiments, have often become unintelligible and consequently useless.

How could modern philosophers, who, under pain of cruel persecution, were commanded to renounce reason, and to subject it to faith, that is, to the authority of priests; how, I say, could men, thus bound, give free scope to their genius, improve reason, and accelerate the progress of the human mind? It was with fear and trembling that even the greatest men obtained a glimpse of truth; rarely had they the courage to announce it; and those, who did, were terribly punished. With Religion, it has ever been unlawful to think, or to combat the prejudices of which man is every where the victim and the dupe.

205. Every man, sufficiently intrepid to announce truths to the world, is sure of incurring the hatred of the ministers of Religion, who loudly call to their aid secular powers; and want the assistance of laws to support both their arguments and their gods. Their clamours expose too evidently the weakness of their cause.

"None call for aid but those who feel distressed."

In Religion, man is not permitted to err. In general, those who err are pitied, and some kindness is shewn to persons who discover new truths; but, when Religion is thought to be interested either in the errors or the discoveries, a holy zeal is kindled, the populace become frantic, and nations are in an uproar.

Can any thing be more afflicting, than to see public and private felicity depending upon a futile system, which is destitute if principles, founded only on a distempered imagination, and incapable of presenting any thing but words void of sense? In what consists the so much boasted utility of a Religion, which nobody can comprehend, which continually torments those who are weak enough to meddle with it, which is incapable of rendering men better, and which often makes them consider it meritorious to be unjust and wicked? Is there a folly more deplorable, and more justly to be combated, than that, which far from doing any service to the human race, only makes them blind, delirious, and miserable, by depriving them of Truth, the sole cure for their wretchedness.

206. Religion has ever filled the mind of man with darkness, and kept him in ignorance of his real duties and true interests. It is only by dispelling the clouds and phantoms of Religion, that we shall discover Truth, Reason, and Morality. Religion diverts us from the causes of evils, and from the remedies which nature prescribes; far from curing, it only aggravates, multiplies, and perpetuates them. Let us observe with the celebrated Lord Bolingbroke, that "*theology is the box of Pandora; and if it is impossible to shut it, it is at least useful to inform men, that this fatal box is open*."

THE END.

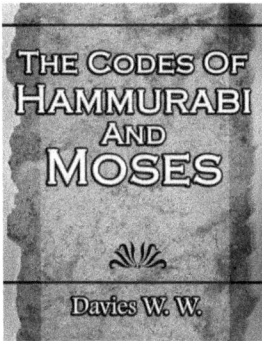

The Codes Of Hammurabi And Moses
W. W. Davies

QTY

The discovery of the Hammurabi Code is one of the greatest achievements of archaeology, and is of paramount interest, not only to the student of the Bible, but also to all those interested in ancient history...

Religion   **ISBN: *1-59462-338-4***   **Pages:132**

MSRP $12.95

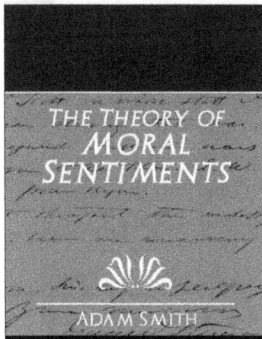

The Theory of Moral Sentiments
Adam Smith

QTY

This work from 1749. contains original theories of conscience amd moral judgment and it is the foundation for systemof morals.

Philosophy   ISBN: *1-59462-777-0*   **Pages:536**

MSRP $19.95

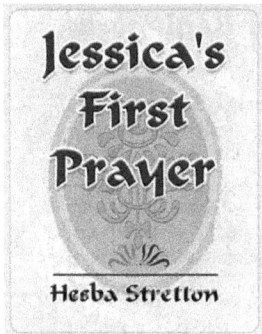

Jessica's First Prayer
Hesba Stretton

QTY

In a screened and secluded corner of one of the many railway-bridges which span the streets of London there could be seen a few years ago, from five o'clock every morning until half past eight, a tidily set-out coffee-stall, consisting of a trestle and board, upon which stood two large tin cans, with a small fire of charcoal burning under each so as to keep the coffee boiling during the early hours of the morning when the work-people were thronging into the city on their way to their daily toil...

Childrens   ISBN: *1-59462-373-2*

Pages:84

MSRP $9.95

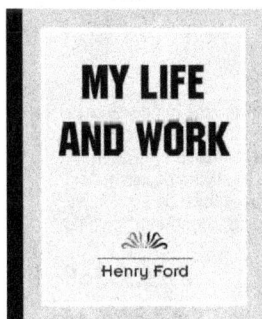

My Life and Work
Henry Ford

QTY

Henry Ford revolutionized the world with his implementation of mass production for the Model T automobile. Gain valuable business insight into his life and work with his own auto-biography... "We have only started on our development of our country we have not as yet, with all our talk of wonderful progress, done more than scratch the surface. The progress has been wonderful enough but..."

Pages:300

Biographies/   ISBN: *1-59462-198-5*   *MSRP $21.95*

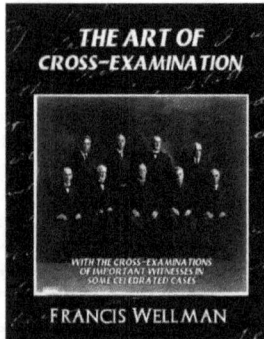

The Art of Cross-Examination
Francis Wellman

QTY

I presume it is the experience of every author, after his first book is published upon an important subject, to be almost overwhelmed with a wealth of ideas and illustrations which could readily have been included in his book, and which to his own mind, at least, seem to make a second edition inevitable. Such certainly was the case with me; and when the first edition had reached its sixth impression in five months, I rejoiced to learn that it seemed to my publishers that the book had met with a sufficiently favorable reception to justify a second and considerably enlarged edition. ..

Pages:412

Reference   ISBN: *1-59462-647-2*   *MSRP $19.95*

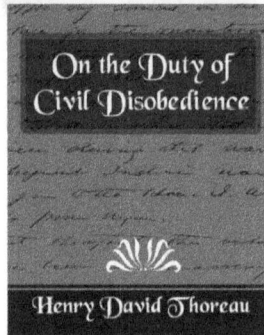

On the Duty of Civil Disobedience
Henry David Thoreau

QTY

Thoreau wrote his famous essay, On the Duty of Civil Disobedience, as a protest against an unjust but popular war and the immoral but popular institution of slave-owning. He did more than write—he declined to pay his taxes, and was hauled off to gaol in consequence. Who can say how much this refusal of his hastened the end of the war and of slavery ?

Law   ISBN: *1-59462-747-9*   **Pages:48**

MSRP $7.45

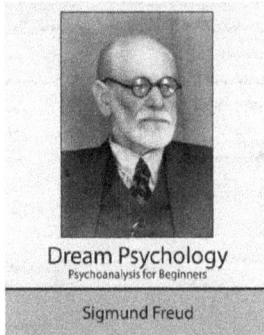

Dream Psychology Psychoanalysis for Beginners
Sigmund Freud

QTY

Sigmund Freud, born Sigismund Schlomo Freud (May 6, 1856 - September 23, 1939), was a Jewish-Austrian neurologist and psychiatrist who co-founded the psychoanalytic school of psychology. Freud is best known for his theories of the unconscious mind, especially involving the mechanism of repression; his redefinition of sexual desire as mobile and directed towards a wide variety of objects; and his therapeutic techniques, especially his understanding of transference in the therapeutic relationship and the presumed value of dreams as sources of insight into unconscious desires.

Pages:196

Psychology   ISBN: *1-59462-905-6*   *MSRP $15.45*

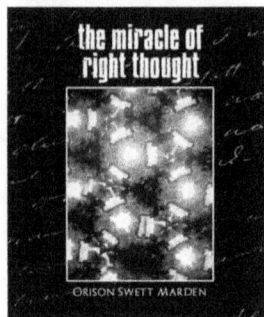

The Miracle of Right Thought
Orison Swett Marden

QTY

Believe with all of your heart that you will do what you were made to do. When the mind has once formed the habit of holding cheerful, happy, prosperous pictures, it will not be easy to form the opposite habit. It does not matter how improbable or how far away this realization may see, or how dark the prospects may be, if we visualize them as best we can, as vividly as possible, hold tenaciously to them and vigorously struggle to attain them, they will gradually become actualized, realized in the life. But a desire, a longing without endeavor, a yearning abandoned or held indifferently will vanish without realization.

Pages:360

Self Help   ISBN: *1-59462-644-8*   *MSRP $25.45*

www.bookjungle.com email: sales@bookjungle.com fax: 630-214-0564 mail: Book Jungle PO Box 2226 Champaign, IL 61825

QTY

The Rosicrucian Cosmo-Conception Mystic Christianity by *Max Heindel* ISBN: *1-59462-188-8* **$38.95**
The Rosicrucian Cosmo-conception is not dogmatic, neither does it appeal to any other authority than the reason of the student. It is: not controversial, but is: sent forth in the, hope that it may help to clear... New Age/Religion Pages 646

Abandonment To Divine Providence by *Jean-Pierre de Caussade* ISBN: *1-59462-228-0* **$25.95**
"The Rev. Jean Pierre de Caussade was one of the most remarkable spiritual writers of the Society of Jesus in France in the 18th Century. His death took place at Toulouse in 1751. His works have gone through many editions and have been republished... Inspirational/Religion Pages 400

Mental Chemistry by *Charles Haanel* ISBN: *1-59462-192-6* **$23.95**
Mental Chemistry allows the change of material conditions by combining and appropriately utilizing the power of the mind. Much like applied chemistry creates something new and unique out of careful combinations of chemicals the mastery of mental chemistry... New Age Pages 354

The Letters of Robert Browning and Elizabeth Barret Barrett 1845-1846 vol II ISBN: *1-59462-193-4* **$35.95**
by *Robert Browning* and *Elizabeth Barrett* Biographies Pages 596

Gleanings In Genesis (volume I) by *Arthur W. Pink* ISBN: *1-59462-130-6* **$27.45**
Appropriately has Genesis been termed "the seed plot of the Bible" for in it we have, in germ form, almost all of the great doctrines which are afterwards fully developed in the books of Scripture which follow... Religion/Inspirational Pages 420

The Master Key by *L. W. de Laurence* ISBN: *1-59462-001-6* **$30.95**
In no branch of human knowledge has there been a more lively increase of the spirit of research during the past few years than in the study of Psychology, Concentration and Mental Discipline. The requests for authentic lessons in Thought Control, Mental Discipline and... New Age/Business Pages 422

The Lesser Key Of Solomon Goetia by *L. W. de Laurence* ISBN: *1-59462-092-X* **$9.95**
This translation of the first book of the "Lemegton" which is now for the first time made accessible to students of Talismanic Magic was done, after careful collation and edition, from numerous Ancient Manuscripts in Hebrew, Latin, and French... New Age/Occult Pages 92

Rubaiyat Of Omar Khayyam by *Edward Fitzgerald* ISBN:*1-59462-332-5* **$13.95**
Edward Fitzgerald, whom the world has already learned, in spite of his own efforts to remain within the shadow of anonymity, to look upon as one of the rarest poets of the century, was born at Bredfield, in Suffolk, on the 31st of March, 1809. He was the third son of John Purcell... Music Pages 172

Ancient Law by *Henry Maine* ISBN: *1-59462-128-4* **$29.95**
The chief object of the following pages is to indicate some of the earliest ideas of mankind, as they are reflected in Ancient Law, and to point out the relation of those ideas to modern thought. Religion/History Pages 452

Far-Away Stories by *William J. Locke* ISBN: *1-59462-129-2* **$19.45**
"Good wine needs no bush, but a collection of mixed vintages does. And this book is just such a collection. Some of the stories I do not want to remain buried for ever in the museum files of dead magazine-numbers an author's not unpardonable vanity..." Fiction Pages 272

Life of David Crockett by *David Crockett* ISBN: *1-59462-250-7* **$27.45**
"Colonel David Crockett was one of the most remarkable men of the times in which he lived. Born in humble life, but gifted with a strong will, an indomitable courage, and unremitting perseverance... Biographies/New Age Pages 424

Lip-Reading by *Edward Nitchie* ISBN: *1-59462-206-X* **$25.95**
Edward B. Nitchie, founder of the New York School for the Hard of Hearing, now the Nitchie School of Lip-Reading, Inc, wrote "LIP-READING Principles and Practice". The development and perfecting of this meritorious work on lip-reading was an undertaking... How-to Pages 400

A Handbook of Suggestive Therapeutics, Applied Hypnotism, Psychic Science ISBN: *1-59462-214-0* **$24.95**
by *Henry Munro* Health/New Age/Health/Self-help Pages 376

A Doll's House: and Two Other Plays by *Henrik Ibsen* ISBN: *1-59462-112-8* **$19.95**
Henrik Ibsen created this classic when in revolutionary 1848 Rome. Introducing some striking concepts in playwriting for the realist genre, this play has been studied the world over. Fiction/Classics/Plays 308

The Light of Asia by *sir Edwin Arnold* ISBN: *1-59462-204-3* **$13.95**
In this poetic masterpiece, Edwin Arnold describes the life and teachings of Buddha. The man who was to become known as Buddha to the world was born as Prince Gautama of India but he rejected the worldly riches and abandoned the reigns of power when... Religion/History/Biographies Pages 170

The Complete Works of Guy de Maupassant by *Guy de Maupassant* ISBN: *1-59462-157-8* **$16.95**
"For days and days, nights and nights, I had dreamed of that first kiss which was to consecrate our engagement, and I knew not on what spot I should put my lips..." Fiction/Classics Pages 240

The Art of Cross-Examination by *Francis L. Wellman* ISBN: *1-59462-309-0* **$26.95**
Written by a renowned trial lawyer, Wellman imparts his experience and uses case studies to explain how to use psychology to extract desired information through questioning. How-to/Science/Reference Pages 408

Answered or Unanswered? by *Louisa Vaughan* ISBN: *1-59462-248-5* **$10.95**
Miracles of Faith in China Religion Pages 112

The Edinburgh Lectures on Mental Science (1909) by *Thomas* ISBN: *1-59462-008-3* **$11.95**
This book contains the substance of a course of lectures recently given by the writer in the Queen Street Hall, Edinburgh. Its purpose is to indicate the Natural Principles governing the relation between Mental Action and Material Conditions... New Age/Psychology Pages 148

Ayesha by *H. Rider Haggard* ISBN: *1-59462-301-5* **$24.95**
Verily and indeed it is the unexpected that happens! Probably if there was one person upon the earth from whom the Editor of this, and of a certain previous history, did not expect to hear again... Classics Pages 380

Ayala's Angel by *Anthony Trollope* ISBN: *1-59462-352-X* **$29.95**
The two girls were both pretty, but Lucy who was twenty-one who supposed to be simple and comparatively unattractive, whereas Ayala was credited, as her Bombwhat romantic name might show, with poetic charm and a taste for romance. Ayala when her father died was nineteen... Fiction Pages 484

The American Commonwealth by *James Bryce* ISBN: *1-59462-286-8* **$34.45**
An interpretation of American democratic political theory. It examines political mechanics and society from the perspective of Scotsman James Bryce Politics Pages 572

Stories of the Pilgrims by *Margaret P. Pumphrey* ISBN: *1-59462-116-0* **$17.95**
This book explores pilgrims religious oppression in England as well as their escape to Holland and eventual crossing to America on the Mayflower, and their early days in New England... History Pages 268

QTY

The Fasting Cure by *Sinclair Upton*   ISBN: *1-59462-222-1* **$13.95**
In the Cosmopolitan Magazine for May, 1910, and in the Contemporary Review (London) for April, 1910, I published an article dealing with my experi-
ences in fasting. I have written a great many magazine articles, but never one which attracted so much attention... New Age/Self Help/Health Pages 164

Hebrew Astrology by *Sepharial*   ISBN: *1-59462-308-2* **$13.45**
In these days of advanced thinking it is a matter of common observation that we have left many of the old landmarks behind and that we are now pressing
forward to greater heights and to a wider horizon than that which represented the mind-content of our progenitors... Astrology Pages 144

Thought Vibration or The Law of Attraction in the Thought World   ISBN: *1-59462-127-6* **$12.95**

by *William Walker Atkinson*   Psychology/Religion Pages 144

Optimism by *Helen Keller*   ISBN: *1-59462-108-X* **$15.95**
Helen Keller was blind, deaf, and mute since 19 months old, yet famously learned how to overcome these handicaps, communicate with the world, and
spread her lectures promoting optimism. An inspiring read for everyone... Biographies/Inspirational Pages 84

Sara Crewe by *Frances Burnett*   ISBN: *1-59462-360-0* **$9.45**
In the first place, Miss Minchin lived in London. Her home was a large, dull, tall one, in a large, dull square, where all the houses were alike, and all the
sparrows were alike, and where all the door-knockers made the same heavy sound... Childrens/Classic Pages 88

The Autobiography of Benjamin Franklin by *Benjamin Franklin*   ISBN: *1-59462-135-7* **$24.95**
The Autobiography of Benjamin Franklin has probably been more extensively read than any other American historical work, and no other book of its kind
has had such ups and downs of fortune. Franklin lived for many years in England, where he was agent... Biographies/History Pages 332

Name	
Email	
Telephone	
Address	
City, State ZIP	

☐ **Credit Card**   ☐ **Check / Money Order**

Credit Card Number	
Expiration Date	
Signature	

Please Mail to: Book Jungle
PO Box 2226
Champaign, IL 61825
or Fax to: 630-214-0564

ORDERING INFORMATION

web*: www.bookjungle.com*
email*: sales@bookjungle.com*
fax*: 630-214-0564*
mail*: Book Jungle PO Box 2226 Champaign, IL 61825*
or PayPal *to sales@bookjungle.com*

Please contact us for bulk discounts

DIRECT-ORDER TERMS

**20% Discount if You Order
Two or More Books**
Free Domestic Shipping!
Accepted: Master Card, Visa,
Discover, American Express

www.ingramcontent.com/pod-product-compliance
Lightning Source LLC
Chambersburg PA
CBHW081232090426
42738CB00016B/3267